A Guide to
Oriental
Ceramics

A Guide to
Oriental
Ceramics

Elizabeth
Wilson

Charles E. Tuttle Company
Rutland, Vermont & Tokyo, Japan

Cover photograph: Brian Boyle
Photographs: Brian Boyle, Royal Ontario Museum, pages 35, 36, 73–89
Balangay photograph: Ray A. Santiago, National Museum of the
    Philippines Regional Museum, Butuan, Mindanao
Santa Ana site photograph: Jose Sarmiento, Oriental Photographic and
    Equipment Corporation, Manila
Other photographs: Vito Ongleo, pages 40, 105, 107; Mary Stephen,
    page 76
Illustrations: Joe Figarola

Published by the Charles E. Tuttle Co., Inc.
of Rutland, Vermont & Tokyo, Japan
with editorial offices at
1-2-6 Suido, Bunkyo-ku, Tokyo 112

LCC Card No. 91-65058
ISBN 0-8048-1683-2

First edition, 1991

Printed in Japan

CONTENTS

Color illustrations appear on pages 73–88.

PREFACE

Learning about Asian ceramics was, for me, a daunting task. Study groups and lectures were intimidating because, much of the time, the experts used unfamiliar terms—saggar, cavetto, Yue-type, chocolate bottom. I often found myself trying to compare two similar but slightly different dishes. Do Song pieces or Yuan pieces have glaze on the base? Is a white dish with a greenish tinge more valuable than a milky-white dish? How do you judge the worth? Even though I have been looking at ceramics most of my life, there seemed always far too much to remember.

I also had trouble relating what I read about ceramics to the way I actually looked at them. Antique Asian ceramics are usually displayed in stores and museums according to their color, style, or shape. Blue-and-white pieces are on one shelf, brown jars on another, and celadon ware on a third. Displays are rarely by country of origin or time of making. They are seldom titled Vietnamese, Korean, or fourteenth-century Chinese, for example. Yet that is the way most books classify ceramics.

That is where this book is different. With it in your hand, one piece is easy to compare with a similar piece, perhaps from a different country or time. Celadon is all in one section. So is blue-and-white ware, and so is brown ware. You will be able to see the differences between a green bowl made in Thailand in the fifteenth century and one made in China in the fourteenth, between a fifteenth-century blue-and-white plate from Vietnam and a similar piece from China.

I have concentrated on the shapes and styles that were commonly traded in southeast Asia from the tenth to the seventeenth centuries. Ceramics that were not much exported are usually described only in the section called **Talking Ceramics**. This is also true of styles not often found in shops in southeast Asia. For example, Chinese Tang and Yue wares are not dealt with in detail since they are generally enjoyed more in museums and private collections than in shops and small galleries. Yue-type ware is discussed because there are many pieces on the market. To learn more about these and other styles of ceramics, consult the reading list at the end.

This book is designed to fit easily into a pocket or bag, so it can be carried along on ceramics expeditions. The guide to where to look for ceramics, and what to look for there, should whet the appetite and overcome the shyness of newcomers. A caution: ceramics are as variable as any artifacts. Descriptions in any book will be correct most, but by no means all, of the time. It should also be kept in mind that most of the descriptions apply to export ware and not necessarily to the whole production in a particular style. Discoveries are being made all the time in many countries, both in Asia and in the Middle East. New theories are announced every year about the origins of different wares. As a result, opinion changes, and so does the terminology. More and more, people talk about the area, even the kiln site, from which a piece comes. Less and less do they identify pieces only by general style, or by country or period. Attribution of Chinese pieces always waits upon research in China. People in other countries may have ideas, but cannot be sure until the Chinese announce their results.

The book begins with an illustrated glossary, **Talking Ceramics,** because you will need to know the language. Don't worry too much about spelling. There are several correct ways to spell many of the Asian names in English. I have given the names in Pinyin, the official style of modern China. Other spellings are also given in the section **Talking Ceramics.** A bit of history follows to acquaint the beginner with what was happening in China during each dynasty, and in Thailand and Vietnam during the time these countries exported ceramics. The relationships between Chinese, Thai, Vietnamese, Korean, and Japanese ceramics—the similarities in style, the trading patterns—are also described.

After the Explorations section, there are pages for personal notes.

Many of the books in the reading list have been useful in writing this book and I owe their authors a great debt. Even more, I thank the Museum Volunteers of the Philippines, and the Oriental Ceramic Society of the Philippines, Inc., for the education I received at their study groups and for the special help of Society members Rita Tan and Cynthia Valdes. Joan Bacon in Singapore helped research the ceramic market in Southeast Asia. Patricia Proctor of the Royal Ontario Museum Far Eastern Department assisted me in every possible way, introducing me to the excellent study collection and providing a detailed commentary on the final text. The pieces in the photographs are from my own collection, other private collections, and the Royal Ontario Museum.

Finally, thanks to Susan Hargrove, who gave me the idea, and to my husband and best critic, Ian Montagnes. Thanks are also due to the Charles E. Tuttle Co., Inc., and its excellent editorial staff.

Elizabeth Wilson
Toronto, Canada

ORIENTATION

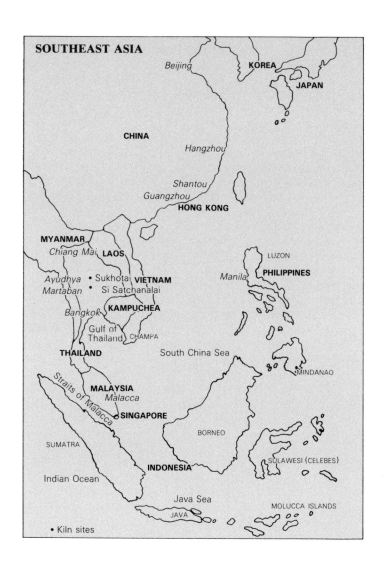

SOUTHEAST ASIA

Beijing

KOREA

JAPAN

CHINA

Hangzhou

Shantou

Guangzhou

HONG KONG

MYANMAR

Chiang Mai LAOS

LUZON

Ayudhya • Sukhotai VIETNAM

Manila PHILIPPINES

Martaban • Si Satchanalai

Bangkok KAMPUCHEA

Gulf of
Thailand CHAMPA

THAILAND

South China Sea

MINDANAO

Straits of Malacca

MALAYSIA
Malacca

SINGAPORE

BORNEO

SUMATRA

SULAWESI (CELEBES)

INDONESIA

Indian Ocean

Java Sea

MOLUCCA ISLANDS

JAVA

• Kiln sites

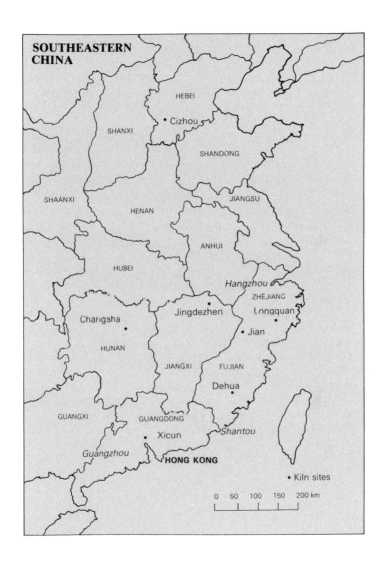

SOUTHEASTERN CHINA

HEBEI

• Cizhou

SHANXI

SHANDONG

SHAANXI

JIANGSU

HENAN

ANHUI

HUBEI

Hangzhou

ZHEJIANG

Jingdezhen

Longquan

Changsha

Jian

HUNAN

JIANGXI

FUJIAN

Dehua

GUANGXI

GUANGDONG

Xicun

Shantou

Guangzhou

HONG KONG

• Kiln sites

0 50 100 150 200 km

IMPORTANT DATES

China
Tang (T'ang) dynasty	AD 618–907
Five dynasties	907–960
Song (Sung) dynasty	960–1271
Northern Song	960–1127
Southern Song	1127–1271
Yuan dynasty	1271–1368
Ming dynasty	1368–1644
Qing (Ch'ing, Manchu) dynasty	1644–1911

Indonesia
Srivijaya empire	600–1200
Majapahit empire	1200–1500

Japan
Heian period	794–1185
Kamakura period	1185–1336
Muromachi period	1336–1568
Momoyama period	1568–1603
Edo period	1603–1868

Kampuchea (Cambodia)
Major ceramic period	900–1250

Korea
Koryo dynasty	918–1392
Yi dynasty	1392–1910

Philippines
Coming of the Spanish	1521

Thailand
Sawankhalok ware	1350–1500
Sukhotai ware	1350–1500

Vietnam
Early export	1200–1400
Middle export	1400–1600
Late export	1600–1700

TALKING CERAMICS

Jar

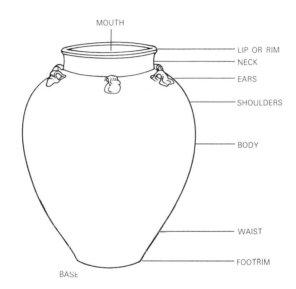

MOUTH

LIP OR RIM
NECK
EARS
SHOULDERS

BODY

WAIST

FOOTRIM

BASE

Bowl

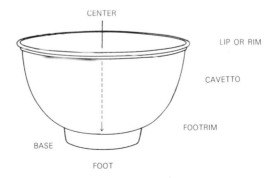

CENTER

LIP OR RIM

CAVETTO

FOOTRIM

BASE

FOOT

GLOSSARY

anhua   Secret decoration. Finely incised lines or very low relief that are difficult to see. First appeared on Chinese white ware in the fifteenth century.

Annam   Old Chinese name for the northern part of Vietnam.

applied decoration   A separately shaped piece of clay added to the basic form; for example, a pair of molded fish on some celadon plates, or dragons on some water jars (Plate 17).

Arita ware   First Japanese porcelain ware. Made from the early seventeenth century in Arita on the island of Kyushu by Korean immigrants. Much of the initial production was blue-and-white ware. Overglaze enameling came later.

balimbing   The Philippine name for a fruit with triangular facets, also known as a star fruit. The name is given to the shape of small jars made primarily for the Philippine market.

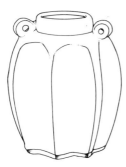

Balimbing jarlet

Bencharong ware Multicolored ware from China made for the Thai market, especially in the Qing dynasty.

beading A raised line in the form of a string of small beads. This style of decoration began in the Yuan period. It is often found on *qingbai* pieces and on blue-and-white ware.

biscuit / bisque Unglazed pottery that has been fired, likely just once. It may be fragile. The term is also used to describe the body underneath a glaze.

black-and-white ware Ceramics with black or dark brown decoration on a white or off-white body. The usual descriptive term is underglaze black. Much of this ware is Vietnamese or Thai. Several styles, often with large, solid black decoration, were also produced in China (See ***underglaze black***).

blanc-de-chine ware Pure white porcelain with a smooth glaze made since the sixteenth century at the Dehua kilns in Fujian province, China. Small figures of Buddha and Guanyin, the goddess of mercy, are common.

box Small pot or dish, usually with a lid. Often round or hexagonal.

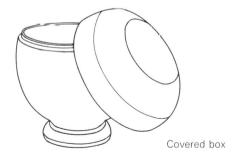

Covered box

Canton See *Guangzhou.*

Canton ware Roughly decorated blue-and-white ware, late Qing, made in and around Canton (Guangzhou). Pieces have an unglazed ring in the center so they would not stick together when stacked in the kiln. Also called Hong Kong, Kitchen Ming, Kitchen Qing, or Singapore ware (Plate 22).

carving Designs of leaves, flowers, scrolls, etc. cut into the damp clay with a broad tool (Plate 13).

cavetto The sloping sides of a bowl or deep dish. Also called the "well."

celadon Green ware made by adding a small amount of iron oxide to the glaze. While called "green ware," it may be yellow, grey, turquoise, or bluish. See the *Yue/celadon/green ware* section (Plates 6–13b).

ceramic Object made of fired clay.

Champa ware Ceramics from the area that is now central Vietnam.

Changsha ware Stoneware with buff body and a clear glaze of greenish or yellowish tint. One style has molded medallions splashed with dark brown glaze. Late Tang. Made in Hunan province, China (Plate 1).

Chaoan ware Green ware and *qingbai* produced in a county by that name in Guangdong province, China, from the twelfth century.

Chekiang See *Zhejiang.*

Chi-chou See *Jizhou.*

Chien See *Jian.*

Ching-pai ware See *qingbai.*

Ching-te-chen   See *Jingdezhen.*

chocolate bottom   Brown painted base found on about one-third of known Vietnamese export pieces. A small number of Thai pieces also have this decoration. The purpose is unknown (Plate 19b).

Cizhou (Tz'u-chou) ware   Popular ware produced in many northern Chinese kilns in the Song periods. It marks the first appearance of decoration painted over a white slip and under a clear glaze. Cizhou ware has many decorative styles and techniques. Usually the pieces have a floral, free style of decoration and a bold pattern in black or brown. Some export.

cobalt   The blue pigment used to decorate blue-and-white ware.

combing   Dot or line decoration made by pressing a comb into damp clay or by dragging a comb across the clay.

crackle / crazing   A fine network of cracks in the glaze. Crackle occurs when the glaze and the body expand or contract at different rates. A potter may let outside air enter the kiln suddenly instead of allowing pieces to cool gradually after firing. Intentional crackle is sometimes artificially darkened to accentuate the pattern.

Dehua (Te-hua) ware   White ware from kilns in Fujian province, China. Pieces from the fourteenth century have been found in southeast Asia. Called Marco Polo ware because he is reputed to have brought a piece back to Venice from the Mongol court. Beginning in the sixteenth century the Dehua kilns went on to make *blanc de chine,* a pure white porcelain with a smooth glaze (Plates 14a, 14b).

Ding (Ting) ware   Song porcelaneous stoneware from

Hebei province in China. Superior quality, perhaps imperial ware. Pieces have warm, cream color. They usually have molded or incised decoration. The rim is unglazed and often has a metal binding. Not exported.

earthenware   Pottery made from common clay, sometimes called terra cotta, fired at a low temperature (800–1100°C). White or pink or grey. Earthenware was not glazed in primitive societies.

enamel   A mixture of pigments and silicate applied over the biscuit or the glaze.

Famille jaune, noire, rose, or verte   Ming- and Qing-period Chinese porcelains with enamel decoration. Associated with porcelain exported to Europe.

fired   Baked in a hot oven or kiln. High firing (1200–1400°C) is used for porcelain, moderate firing (1200–1280°C) is used for stoneware, low firing (800–1100°C) for earthenware.

footrim   The round rim carved into the foot of the piece. It is made by turning the partly dry piece upside down, trimming it so that it stands squarely, and carving the clay away from the center of the base, leaving a rim upon which the piece can sit.

Fujian (Fukien)   Province in south China.

glaze   A liquid mineral coating that becomes glassy when heated, used to decorate and seal the surface of pottery. A piece may be dipped in glaze before firing, or the glaze may be painted or blown on in a fine spray.

gourd, single or double   Small pots, or teapots with small handles and stubby spouts. May have one lobe or two.

green ware   Stoneware with a glaze containing iron oxide. See *celadon*.

guan (kuan)   Large jar with a wide mouth and high shoulders, sometimes with a lid. Often blue-and-white ware.

Guan ware   Chinese Imperial ware made in the Southern Song period. Not exported. Thin dark body, thick glaze, heavy crackle. It is hard to tell the age of a piece because many copies were made in the eighteenth century and later. These were exported.

Guangdong (Kuangtung)   Province in south China.

Guangzhou   Capital of Guangdong province, China. Long known in English as Canton, whence derives the name Canton ware.

Guanyin (Kuan-yin)   The deity of compassion and mercy, usually represented as a god in India (Avalokiteshvara) and a goddess in China and Japan (Kannon).

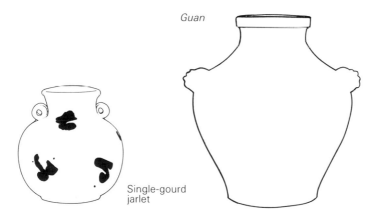

Guan

Single-gourd jarlet

hare's-fur glaze Pattern of fine brown streaks found on Jian black ware from Fujian province, China. Song dynasty (Plate 2).

heirloom piece A piece that has been passed down through a family and never buried.

high-fired See ***fired***.

hole-bottom A deeply recessed glazed base surrounded by a roughly finished unglazed area, found on some small blue-and-white saucers that have no footrim. The purpose of the recess is unknown. Hole-bottom pieces often have an unglazed fish in the center. First made in China in the early Ming period.

Hong Kong ware See ***Canton ware***.

Ido The Japanese name for a type of Yi-dynasty Korean bowls. Much favored in Japan as tea bowls.

Imari ware Japanese enameled porcelain produced in Arita beginning around 1600. Named for the port of Imari, whence it was shipped to other parts of Japan, including Nagasaki. Dutch merchants there exported it to southeast Asia and Europe in the late seventeenth and early eighteenth centuries.

impressed design See ***stamping***.

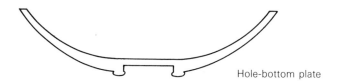

Hole-bottom plate

incised design   Decoration of leaves, flowers, scrolls, lines cut into damp clay with a fine wooden or bamboo stick (Plate 15).

jarlet   Small, squat, rounded, or square jar with a small mouth. Vietnamese or Chinese. Because pieces this small are hard to form on a wheel, jarlets were usually made in two parts. The lower part was luted to a separately formed upper part. The line resulting from the join can be felt by running a finger inside the jarlet around the shoulder.

Jian ware   Famous domestic black ware produced in Fujian province, likely in the Song period. Known for hare's-fur glaze, usually applied to tea bowls (Plate 2). Best known by the Japanese name *temmoku*.

Jingdezhen (Ching-te-chen)   City in Jiangxi province in south China where porcelain was perfected and largely produced. Fine porcelains were produced there throughout the Ming and Qing dynasties. As far as is yet known, Yuan blue-and-white ware was made only in Jingdezhen.

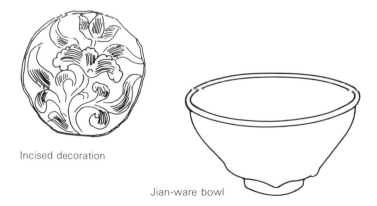

Incised decoration

Jian-ware bowl

Jizhou (Chi-chou) ware Popular ware produced in Jiangxi province in China in the Song period. Tea bowls are the most common pieces. Underglaze painted decoration is similar to the Cizhou style. The names are often confused.

Jun (Chun) ware Made in a number of kilns in Henan, China, beginning in the Song period. Distinctive thick medium-blue glaze often has purply red splashes. Not exported.

Kalong ware Products of major Thai ceramic center. Underglaze black and soft grey monochrome are most common.

Kampuchea Cambodia; also known as Khmer.

Karatsu ware Japanese utilitarian ware from the Momoyama period. Light rice-straw ash glazes and dark iron glazes predominate.

kendi Water jar with a spout and, usually, no handle.

Kendi

Khmer Kampuchea; also known as Cambodia.

kiln Furnace or oven for making pottery. Kilns were fueled in ancient times by wood or coal. Modern kilns are usually fired by gas or electricity.

kiln waster Substandard piece. May be misshapen, have a defective glaze, or in some other way have been damaged in the firing.

Kitchen Ming ware See ***Canton ware.***

Kitchen Qing ware See ***Canton ware.***

Koryo The Korean dynasty (918–1392) during which the best Korean celadon ware was produced.

Kraak porcelain Sixteenth–seventeenth century Chinese blue-and-white porcelain mostly exported to Europe. Likely named after the type of Portuguese craft that transported ceramics in southeast Asia.

kuan See ***guan.***

Kuangtung See ***Guangdong.***

Koryo celadon bowl

lighthouse support   A tall cylindrical support on which Sawankhalok potters placed ceramic pieces during firing. Many Sawankhalok pieces have a brown ring on the base where the piece was attached with resin to the support.

Longquan (Lung-ch'uan)   A large group of kilns in Zhejiang province, south China, the source of the finest celadons. Longquan and its imitators dominated celadon production from the Song to the Ming periods.

lotus jar   Ribbed covered jar with an undulating lid. Chinese; usually Yuan period.

luting   Joining two pieces of moist clay with runny clay. Luting is found at the shoulders of many jars and jarlets. The join can be felt by running a finger inside around the shoulder. Luting is common at the widest part of rounded boxes or dishes. The rims of large plates are often added to the basic form by luting.

mangosteen   Small round dark–skinned Asian fruit. Some Sawankhalok boxes are shaped like mangosteens. The

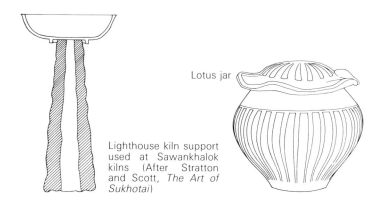

Lotus jar

Lighthouse kiln support used at Sawankhalok kilns (After Stratton and Scott, *The Art of Sukhotai*)

very distinctive stalk and calyx are often depicted on the lid.

Marco Polo ware See ***Dehua ware.***

Martab(v)an jar Large, earthenware jar, usually brown, but may be green, blue, white, or several colors. Some are plain; others are decorated with applied flying dragons. Many have small loop handles at the shoulder or close to the neck. Martaban is a port in Burma, from which these Chinese jars were transported from the Song to the Qing dynasties.

Meiping vase Tall vase with rounded shoulders and a narrow mouth and base, often seen in blue-and-white ware.

molded design Decoration on a ceramic piece made by pressing it, while still damp, on to a mold.

Nanhai trade Commerce between China and southeast Asian countries, India, and the Middle East. "Nanhai" means "South Seas."

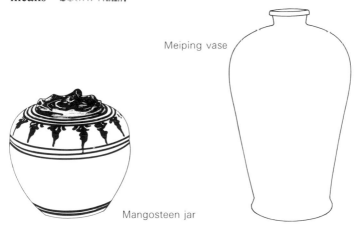

Meiping vase

Mangosteen jar

Nonya ware Ceramics made in Jingdezhen, China, in the late nineteenth and early twentieth centuries for ceremonial use by Chinese families living near the Straits of Malacca. Multicolored enamel decoration.

overglaze Color applied after the piece has already had at least one layer of glaze applied. Many overglaze pieces on the market have been repainted. See also *underglaze.*

paste Clay body, exclusive of the glaze.

peony Major Chinese decorative element. Symbol of happiness, wealth, love, and spring.

pontil Support on which the base of a ceramic piece rests during firing.

pooling Darker color, formed when streams of glaze run together to form a pool.

porcelain Especially fine kind of pottery, fired at a very high temperature. Usually high quality, hard, dense, white, non-porous, and, if thin, translucent. Porcelain rings when struck. The Chinese use the last characteristic to define the term.

Peony spray

porcelain, Chinese export Usual phrase for pieces made in the Ming and Qing dynasties for a non-Asian market. Styles and colors are often referred to in French, as, e.g., *famille rose.*

porcelaneous stoneware High-fired white ware, but not as glassy as true porcelain.

potting Forming of a pot, usually on a potter's wheel.

potting, unrefined Pieces that are unsatisfactory in their forming. The base may be rough, the shaping and finishing uneven, or the piece too heavy for its size.

proto-Yue ware See *Yue ware.*

Punch'ong (powder-green) ware Korean domestic ware. Plain, molded, or incised. Yi period. Influenced Japanese ceramic styles.

qingbai (Ch'ing-pai) ware White ware with a pale bluish glaze. Made in southern China in the Song and Yuan dynasties. Also called *yingqing* (Plate 15).

Raku ware Japanese earthenware made from the sixteenth century on. Straight-sided bowls used in tea ceremony.

relief decoration A small piece of clay attached to a piece as decoration. Often takes the form of a fish, person, or flower. The relief may or may not be decorated (Plate 11).

rice-grain decoration An eighteenth-century style of decoration used on blue-and-white ware. Openings the size of a grain of rice are cut through the body. The holes are then filled in with glaze.

rim, everted A rim that is turned outward.

rim, foliated   A rim whose edge undulates in the shape of leaves; sometimes used to disguise possible distortion during firing, sometimes for decoration.

rim, lobed   A rim that has regularly spaced nicks dividing it into sections.

saggar   Box of baked, fireproof clay used to enclose and protect pieces during firing.

sang-de-boeuf ware   A deep, glowing red monochrome ware. Chinese. Especially fine in the early Qing period.

Satsuma ware (brocaded)   Made from the late eighteenth century in Japan, primarily for export to the Western market. Heavily decorated with enamel and gold over a transparent glaze on a cream-colored body.

Satsuma ware (original)   Japanese stoneware with black and/or brown glaze. Used both for domestic purposes and for the tea ceremony. Made in Satsuma province by Korean potters, from the late sixteenth century on.

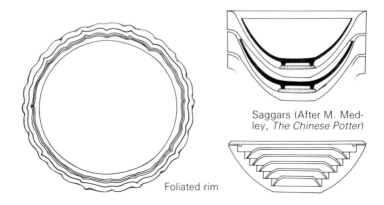

Saggars (After M. Medley, *The Chinese Potter*)

Foliated rim

Sawankhalok ware Ceramics made at a group of kilns near Si Satchanalai, Thailand, from the mid-fourteenth to the beginning of the sixteenth centuries.

Shantou (Swatow) ware Ming and Qing ware from kilns in southern China; named after the port in southeast China from which much of it was shipped. Usually blue-and-white, but may be decorated in red, green, turquoise, or black enamels (Plates 23a, 23b).

shard/sherd Fragment of broken pottery, often used to identify the origins of a group of ceramics, since the composition of the clay is visible (Plate 6).

Shufu ware Porcelains with a rather matt, milky glaze produced in Jingdezhen during the Yuan period.

Singapore ware See *Canton ware.*

Si Satchanalai Site of Sawankhalok kilns in Thailand.

slip Watery clay used to coat a piece before glazing or decorating. Slip fills in small holes, provides a smooth surface for decorating, and enhances the color of the glaze.

spotted ware Pieces with brown spots or splotches on a celadon or *qingbai* ground. The spots were often used to cover up defects, especially in celadon pieces; in *qingbai* ware, they seem more often to be simply for decoration. The technique started with proto-Yue ware.

spur marks Symmetrically placed small marks in the center or on the base. They were made by the small stands with raised sections, or spurs, that were used to separate pieces during firing.

stamping Design stamped into damp clay with a mold. This method of decorating ceramics is faster than incising. Also called impressing (Plate 13).

stem cup   Bowl raised on a tall, hollow base that is wider at the bottom than the top.

stoneware   Pottery fired in a hot kiln (1200–1280°C), hard, non-porous, and durable. If the body is colored, the piece is stoneware or earthenware. If the body is white, but not glassy or dense, it is probably stoneware. Pieces are usually glazed. Often difficult to tell from porcelain, although stoneware is usually thicker and less translucent than porcelain.

Sukhotai ware   Pieces made at a group of kilns in Thailand. They were active from the mid-fourteenth to the beginning of the sixteenth centuries.

Swatow ware   See *Shantou ware.*

Te Hua ware   See *Dehua ware.*

temmoku ware   Japanese term applied to Song-dynasty wares with a thick, shiny, brown or black glaze and, sometimes, hare's-fur streaks, or iridescent or oil spots (Plate 2). Often seen in rounded tea bowls. Most *temmoku*-type ware seen in southeast Asia was made in Jian, Fujian province, or in Jiangxi or Guangdong provinces in China.

Stem cups

terra cotta   Brownish-red earthenware or color.

transitional ware   In blue-and-white ware, this term describes porcelains made just at the end of the Ming and the beginning of the Qing dynasties. In white ware, it describes the transition from the simplicity of Song ware to the molded and blue-and-white decoration of the Yuan dynasty.

Tz'u-chou ware   See *Cizhou ware.*

underglaze   Decoration painted on a clay piece before glazing and firing. The piece required only one firing.

vitrify   To convert clay into a hard, glass-like substance by firing it at above 1250°C.

waster   See *kiln waster.*

water dropper   Miniature vessel used by Chinese scholars for pouring water onto the inkstone used in making ink for calligraphy and other brushwork. The term is now used for any piece with a spout and no obvious purpose (Plate 5).

willow pattern   An early nineteenth-century English transfer pattern showing a Chinese landscape in blue-and-white. Later produced in China for export to the West.

wire-cut bottom   Flat bottom created by slipping a thin wire under the piece to separate it from the potter's wheel.

wreathing marks   Horizontal ridges up the side of a pot made by the potter's hands as the piece is shaped. These ridges are usually smoothed over or scraped off by the potter.

Xicun (Hsi-ts'un)   Major kiln site near Guangzhou,

China. Active in Northern Song period. Major exporter of green ware with carved or impressed decoration.

Yingqing See ***qingbai.***

Yixing (I-hsing) ware Chinese unglazed stoneware. Fine, reddish-brown. Mostly teapots. Sixteenth century to present. Geometric shapes are the most common but many pieces are shaped like plants or tree trunks. Often technically superb.

Yue ware A type of Chinese green ware produced during the seventh to the tenth centuries; a similar type known as proto-Yue ware was produced from the fourth century. The best pieces were made in Wu Yue in northern Zhejiang province.

Zhejiang (Chekiang) Province in southeast China, north of Fujian province.

Yixing teapot

WATCH THE BOTTOM LINE

In looking critically at any piece, the bottom is a good place to begin. The base and the footrim tell a lot about the age, origin, and even the kiln of a ceramic piece. Sometimes the shape and finish of the bottom may be all the clues you need. Start with the bases in this book, especially in the color section.

The base and footrim are the last parts to be fashioned. While the finished piece is still partly dry, it is turned upside down and trimmed so that it will stand squarely. With tools, the potter carves the clay away around the foot and base, leaving a rim around the bottom. If the inner part of the rim were not trimmed away and the base were to be left much thicker than the rest, it would take longer to fire and the piece might break or crack. Carving away some of the clay makes the pot roughly the same thickness all over.

The foot is usually shaped while the piece revolves on the potter's wheel. It may be made square or rounded at the bot-

Base of Yue-type bowl

Base of Northern Song small celadon bowl. Clay is gray. Glazed footrim.

tom. It may be wide or very thin, flared or straight, tall or short. The base itself may be deep or shallow, clean or messy, glazed or unglazed. It may have marks made by kiln supports. Each kind of ware has a style all its own (Plates 6, 13, 14, 15, 19, 22, 23). Many Vietnamese pieces, for instance, have a brown wash on the base rarely found elsewhere (Plate 19b).

The way the glaze is applied is important too. The base and foot may be fully or partially glazed. Some pieces look perfectly glazed when viewed from the top but may have sloppily applied glaze on the bottom. Or the potter may have applied glaze only to the upper part of the pot, leaving the base clay exposed (Plate 4).

Base of Sawankhalok covered jar. The glaze does not come down to the base. Brown specks in the center show where the piece was attached to the kiln support.

Base of celadon covered bowl. Only the footrim is unglazed.

CERAMICS IN SOUTHEAST ASIA

The Chinese began exporting ceramics in the first or second centuries AD. By the beginning of the Tang dynasty in the seventh century, ceramics were big business. The wares of northern China were shipped as far as Persia along the famous Silk Road. By the end of the Tang period, southern wares were going by sea to Asian countries and then to the Middle East and North Africa. The seas made pathways for trade, not barriers. Marco Polo, that adventurer and chronicler of the court of Kublai Khan in Cathay (China), wrote that in around 1300, from one region alone, "bowls of porcelain, large and small, of incomparable beauty . . . are exported all over the world." Chinese porcelain and stoneware reached southeast Asia as early as the ninth century. From South China the little ships took one of two routes. Either they went down the west coast of the Philippines past Borneo and Sulawesi to the Molucca Islands, or they followed the coastline of Vietnam, Thailand, and the Malay Peninsula. From there they either turned south to Java and Sumatra or headed west out into the Indian Ocean and, perhaps, the far-off coast of Africa.

The romance of the ancient ceramic trade never fades. An exotic list, indeed, is this official record of a Chinese trader's life in the eleventh century: "[We used] gold, silver, copper coinage, lead, tin, mixed colored silk, and rough and fine porcelain to trade and exchange for aromatic products, rhinoceros horns, coral, amber, pearl, iron, turtle shell, cornelian, giant clam, foreign cloths, ebony, sapanwood and the like."

Later, in the mid-fourteenth century, the Ming emperors brought foreign trade under direct court control. While private trade continued, it was severely restricted for several centuries. Overall, the ceramic trade declined, creating an opportunity that Thai and Vietnamese merchants were quick to exploit. Their ceramics flooded into the Philippines and Indonesia. Burial sites in these countries contain a mixture of Chinese, Thai, and Vietnamese ware. The Thai and the Vietnamese traded with China and with all the other countries in the region. In 1602 the journals of the Dutch East India Company record that 12 million pieces of ceramics were traded by the Chinese, the Thai, the Indonesians, the Portuguese, and the Spanish.

No one would argue that the best products of Chinese kilns came to southeast Asia. The finest pieces were reserved for the Chinese imperial court and for the more lucrative Middle East markets. Nor would anyone argue, as they once did, that overseas customers received only the discards. Many pieces compare favorably with pieces in museums in China or, for that matter, with the antique ceramics displayed nowadays in the best shops in Hong Kong.

Until the fourteenth century, celadon pieces were prized above all others. The best celadons are a rich, glowing green often compared to some types of jade, but many attractive pieces range from gold to olive green to blue-green. In the fifteenth century, people also liked Thai celadon. It is often heavier and less glossy, but its colors can be beautiful. Gradually, however, celadon lost out to the blue-and-white ware produced in China and Vietnam for the Middle East. The Chinese took to the new ware slowly, but the Philippines and Indonesia proved to be the ideal markets for early experiments in glazing techniques.

While most of the exports were celadon and blue-and-white wares, the three main exporting areas shipped great quantities of white ware, white ware with black or brown decoration, plain brown ware, monochrome ware in other colors, and a variety of other ceramics such as white ware with red decoration. Some Khmer ceramics from Kampuchea (Cambodia) also found their way around southeast Asia, but there was no regular trade.

None of these ceramics moved into a vacuum. Each country had its own pottery with a long history and a local style. Yet all the countries shared a common Asian tradition, shaping and decorating their earthenware in much the same way. People were producing rough but strongly and elegantly shaped earthenware for domestic and ceremonial use by at least the second millennium BC. Some plain, low-fired pottery has been dated, using Carbon-14, to almost 6000 BC.

The first pottery was for domestic use. Banana leaves could serve as plates and shells could act as bowls, but pottery was needed where nature provided no more suitable container. Large brown jars were made to hold rice wine and oil. Smaller jars held lime paste for betel, pickles, or herbs. Most cooking pots looked much the same as those used nowadays in country kitchens, with a flared lip and a rounded base that settles well over a fire. Pottery *kendi*, a complex form probably of Indian origin, emerged in

Ban Chiang black, incised ware. Thailand. 3000 B.C.

Philippine earthenware *kendi*. Age unknown. 15 cm high.

southeast Asia as early as the tenth century. *Kendi* are very difficult to make.

People did not want the contents of their jars leaking out through the porous clay. Since early potters had no glazes, they sealed the pores of their clay by polishing the outer surface or by applying slip. Often they added incised or embossed decoration. This is as far as local manufacture developed. As foreign trade grew beginning in the tenth century, local work declined in importance. People preferred the imported Chinese glazed stoneware. It was more durable than the unglazed earthenware and, because it was not porous, it was better for storing most liquids. They also liked the new forms such as wine pots and pieces with feet that could stand squarely.

Local earthenware had long been used in ceremonies as well. It was buried in graves and played a part in the rituals and magic of animistic religions. People believed that the

Philippine earthenware plate. 200 BC–AD 600. 28 cm across.

new imported glazed pieces were even greater talismans to be treated reverently. The uses of both local and imported pottery seem endless: for dowries, at weddings, for bathing, for serving food, at funerals, and at births. People thought that celadon plates would change color if poison food was placed on them, and that plates and bowls could talk, cure diseases, or act as instruments for summoning powerful forces in their religions. The ringing sound made by striking a piece of celadon stoneware was thought to have magic qualities. In South Sulawesi, new-born children of noble families were placed on antique celadon dishes.

Most of the early ceramics found in southeast Asia have been excavated from graves. Furnishing graves is a universal practice among ancient peoples. They believed that earthly life and the afterlife are continuous. Mourners wanted to ensure that the dead lived well and retained the prestige they had on earth. They often put plates, jars, bowls, and figurines at the head and feet of the corpse, a dish beneath each hand, and a large dish over the pubic area. The best pieces were often placed in the graves of children, possibly by doting parents. Large urns were sometimes used to hold the bodies of children and noble persons. Sometimes the pieces were broken as part of the burial rites. More often, objects available to collectors today are chipped or broken from having been dug up too roughly, or because shallow sites were accidently plowed over.

The most lavishly outfitted graves are found close to gold mines, presumably the source of the wealth of the departed. Ceramics are also found in trading centers like Santa Ana in Manila in the Philippines, royal courts such as Srivijaya in Sumatra and Majapahit in Java, and major temples such as Borobudur in Java.

As a result of increasing foreign influences, ancestor worship, and with it grave furnishing, declined in the late sixteenth century except in remote areas. Islam reached Indonesia; the Spanish conquered the Philippines; and the Dutch and the British moved into Malaysia. Thereafter, ceramics generally stayed above ground. Many fine pieces, usually Ming celadon or blue-and-white or Qing blue-and-white, were passed down through families. Now called "heirloom" pieces, they are often in fine condition.

The importance of the China trade diminished gradually. At the end of the Ming period, China was in political disarray. In the early Qing dynasty, the export of ceramics declined and overseas customers started to look to Japan for blue-and-white ware and other styles. In the Philippines, the Spanish discouraged trade with both China and Japan, and the country became more dependent on the galleon

Grave site, Santa Ana, Manila, Philippines

trade with Mexico. Indonesia was a major importer of ceramics from Japan. China did, however, continue to produce in the Qing period enormous quantities of everyday blue-and-white tableware that is often seen today. Chinese potters also produced ceramics for the European market, many of which were also sold in southeast Asia.

Up until the 1960s, the study of all of these ceramics was almost unknown. Gradually, the interest of scholars and col-

Recovering a 13th-century boat that traded Thai, Vietnamese, and Chinese ceramics in Indonesia and the Philippines.

lectors in Asia was aroused. In 1958 Dr. Robert Fox of the Philippine National Museum began the first professional excavations not far from Manila. More than 1,500 graves yielded fourteenth- and fifteenth-century pieces from the three major exporting countries.

Since then excavation has been constant in all southeast Asian countries. Major finds occured in Thailand in 1984, for example. Numerous underglaze black pieces from digs in Northern Thailand and Myanmar have recently appeared on the market. Excavation has also proceeded in China, which has the most to contribute to ceramic study. Everyone eagerly awaits new findings from that country.

In southeast Asia the richest treasures, still to be discovered, lie under the sea. On land, the number of new sites has declined, although pieces are still being excavated. Underwater archeology may become more important than excavation on land, and governments are taking steps to control the theft of treasures by amateur divers.

AGES AND ORIGINS

Chinese Dynasties

Tang Dynasty   (618-907)

The three hundred years of the Tang dynasty were one of the most brilliant periods in all Chinese history. Chinese culture and influence spread through Asia to India and as far as the Persian Gulf. In return, the metalwork, textiles, glass, precious stones, and art objects that poured into China from these countries influenced Chinese ceramic styles.

Before the middle of the eighth century, multicolored glazed earthenware had appeared in leafy green (copper), blue (cobalt), and brown, amber, and yellow (iron)—the colors found on the famous Tang horses. In their modeling, all the figures of both people and animals are extremely life-like. These ceramics are very well known. Their style of multicolored glazing was used only from the end of the seventh century until the middle of the eighth century, but the quantity produced was enormous.

Gradually in this dynasty, both white and colored stoneware became common. Many Tang pieces have wonderful celadon glazes. Almost all Tang ware has a white slip. The glaze does not usually reach the foot. Bowls and jars are rounded; they almost look ready to explode. Toward the end of the Tang period, many pieces had splayed feet.

Tang ware reached all the countries of southeast Asia but not in anything like the quantities shipped in the next few centuries. Changsha ware is a good example (Plate 1).

Bowls and ewers are widely dispersed. Pieces have even been found in Kenya. Many pieces in the Tang style are more likely to have been made later, while the Tang influence continued, or to be more recent copies.

Five Dynasties   (907–60)

The Five Dynasties is a confusing name and it was a confusing time. Five families in the north of China fought each other, giving rise to five successive dynasties. In the south there were ten kingdoms that largely maintained themselves. Despite the unsettled times, China vastly expanded the export markets opened in the late Tang dynasty. Its merchants did not risk the lives of their own people on the high seas. Instead, they relied on Arab and Persian traders.

The greatest quantity and the finest quality of exports during the Five Dynasties period came from the Yue kilns in Zhejiang province. Experts are rarely prepared to proclaim a piece "Five Dynasties," since the period was so short that attribution is very difficult.

Song Dynasty   (960–1271)

When a piece of ceramic ware is identified as Northern or Southern Song, the reference is to a historical period, not to the part of China where the piece was made (Plate 8). For the first century and a half of the Song dynasty, a succession of emperors ruled the whole country from a capital in northern Henan province. The taste of the imperial court dictated the styles during that time. Elegant, sophisticated work came from the same northern kilns that had been producing white ware and northern celadon since the late Tang dynasty.

During this period, overland trade in ceramics declined. Due to harassment by foreign rulers on the northern frontiers of China, the famous Silk Road to the west was considered unsafe, and eventually closed. The quantity of goods shipped along the internal waterways to the southern port of Guangzhou (Canton) increased dramatically. From there, a maritime silk road carried ceramics to southeast Asia, India, and the Middle East. The Nanhai "South Seas" trade grew steadily, encouraged by the government, which needed money to fight the invaders from the north.

By 1127 the Jin (Chin), a tribe from Manchuria, had completed their invasion of the north and driven the court south to Hangzhou in Zhejiang province. The Southern Song period had begun. Southern kilns, already well established in a rising economy, flourished with their new imperial neighbors. The kilns of Zhejiang province became the most important of this later Song period; their celadons were its major product. The neighboring provinces of Fujian and Guangdong also became famous for export wares (Plate 9). The output was enormous. One county alone might have hundreds of kilns, many up to 70 meters long and producing 40,000 pieces in one firing. Most of the Song ceramics exported to southeast Asia came from the kilns of South China.

Yuan Dynasty   (1271–1368)

Around 1210 the Mongols invaded China under Genghis Khan. By 1279, his grandson, Kublai Khan, completed the conquest. The Yuan dynasty was launched. The Mongols had no interest in the artistic development of the ceramics industry, but they recognized it as an excellent source of revenue. The Silk Road reopened. Ceramic output stepped up as the China trade became truly international. Ceramics from south China, especially celadon/green ware, came to dominate the southeast Asian market (Plates 9, 11). Yuan ceramics were more ornate than Song wares, in both style and decoration. Yet mass production continued: 200,000 pieces were often fired at one time.

While celadon dominated during the Yuan period, other important developments were occurring. Much white ware was produced in Jingdezhen in Jiangxi province, which became the most important porcelain producing area in the world. Molding was common on Shufu ware, and blue-and-white ware began its rise to popularity, at first to meet the demand for it from the Middle East.

Experts have suggested that one-third to one half of all the ceramics found so far in southeast Asia are Chinese pieces from the Yuan period.

Ming Dynasty (1368–1644)

The Chinese at last defeated the Mongols and set up a new dynasty. Trade settled down and the demand for blue-and-white ware grew (Plates 22–23b). Once the court gave its patronage to blue-and-white ware, the hesitant Chinese finally began to buy it. Orders came as well from Islamic and Asian markets.

At the same time, the Ming emperor brought foreign trade under direct court control. Smuggling flourished nevertheless, although official exports declined because of too much bureaucracy. Thai and Vietnamese potters and merchants filled the vacuum and increased their share of the Asian and Middle East markets. White ware and underglaze black/brown ware came in volume from Vietnam (Plate 18) and Thailand (Plate 16). The Vietnamese also became skilled at making export blue-and-white ware. Asian pieces moved westward. Examples have been discovered in Egypt and Syria. Great collections are housed in the Topkapi Sarayi Museum in Istanbul and the Archeological Museum in Teheran.

Although the pieces traded in southeast Asia were generally smaller and not as spectacular as those that went west, the great number of ceramics excavated testifies to the size of the industry. The trade reached its peak at the time of the first European conquests in Asia in the sixteenth and seventeenth centuries. From that time, Chinese ceramics began reaching Europe in quantity. Their influence on manufacture and design was immediate.

Qing Dynasty   (1644–1911)

The Manchus conquered China from northeast Manchuria, establishing the last imperial dynasty as well as the great period of ceramic production. Blue and-white ware reached technical perfection, only to lose popularity gradually to wares decorated with several colors (Plates 21, 23).

During the middle Qing period, Europeans came to dominate much of southeast Asia. The Dutch colonized Indonesia, the British took over Malaysia, Singapore, and Hong Kong, the Portuguese controlled Malacca, and the Spanish conquered the Philippines. The Chinese themselves began to look away from local Asian and Middle East markets to even more profitable markets in France, England, Holland, and later the United States. For these new markets, and to some extent for the traditional markets, styles new to the Chinese were developed. Plates, for instance, began to have flat shelves around the edge to put condiments on in the European fashion. "Chinese export ware" is the phrase used to describe pieces known to have been made for the European market. This trade reached its peak in the late eighteenth century, and the pieces are usually considered separately from the Oriental ceramics that were traded mostly in southeast Asia, the Middle East, and Africa, though Chinese export ware is also found in southeast Asia.

During the Qing period, exports to southeast Asia (and to the west) included monochrome and polychrome wares as well as huge quantities of blue-and-white ware (Plate 21). Many colorful, enameled pieces were exported especially to Indonesia and Malaysia. Nonya ware was made for the Chinese people living around the Straits of Malacca, and another colorful style, Bencharong ware, was produced solely for the Thai market. Some export pieces were of excellent quality and are prized today as "heirloom" pieces; others were hastily mass-produced. Shantou (Swatow) ware is a good example of the latter type (Plates 23a, 23b). It is found everywhere in southeast Asia. In Indonesia, it is the largest single group of ceramics.

Thailand

Thai ceramics are generally known by *where* they were made rather than by *when* they were made, which was mostly in the fourteenth and fifteenth centuries (Plates 3, 6, 7, 10, 16). They did not enjoy the prestige in southeast Asia that was enjoyed by Chinese ceramics.

The two major centers, Sawankhalok and Sukhotai, operated at the same time. There were many other kiln sites, especially in the north, but they are not as well known, possibly because the output was smaller or because the products were not shipped south. Recent shipwreck finds and excavations in northern Thailand have increased the known number of pieces tremendously. In the past ten years or so there has been a great deal of digging, both clandestine and legitimate, in several mountainous provinces in northern Thailand near the Burmese border. As a result Chinese ceramics—celadon and blue-and-white wares—and lots of fourteenth- to sixteenth-century Thai underglaze black ware and celadon has appeared on the market, for these unknown people buried ceramics with the ashes of their dead. Most Thais are Buddhists. Since Buddhists do not bury possessions, more Thai ceramics have been found in Indonesia and the Philippines, where other religions prevail, than within the country where they were made.

Sawankhalok Ware   (1350–1500)

More than 130 Sawankhalok kilns have been found so far. They were centered at Si Satchanalai, about 320 km north of Bangkok. Production flourished there from the mid-fourteenth into the sixteenth centuries, but began before that according to a recent Australian archeological expedition to Si Satchanalai. Then, in the early 1500s, something happened to interrupt production. Perhaps a war broke out between Ayudhya and Chiang Mai, the two major centers of the country. Kilns were abandoned in mid-firing, evidence of a hasty departure. By the mid-sixteenth century, Thai wares were no longer being made. Recently, the industries have been redeveloped. The kiln sites are now open to visitors, and attractive modern celadon ware is available on the market.

Most Sawankhalok ware was intended for export to Indonesia, the Philippines, and Borneo. The most common styles have black or brown leafy patterns under a milky glaze (Plate 16) or are monochrome pieces with celadon, white, or brown glaze (Plates 3, 6, 7, 10). There have been more underglaze black or brown boxes found in Indonesia than in Thailand. Their pattern is called "batik" in Indonesia. Antique shops in Jakarta are filled with such pieces. Twenty to forty percent of the ceramics found in graves in the Philippines are from these kilns.

Sawankhalok covered pot

Small stands used by the Sukhotai potters to separate pieces during firing. The feet of the stands leave small marks on the center of pieces stacked in this manner. (After Stratton and Scott, *The Art of Sukhotai*)

Sukhotai Ware

Some 50 km from the Sawankhalok kilns, the Sukhotai kilns were producing wares in quite different styles. These pottery works were the largest in the world outside China. While Sawankhalok potteries boasted a wide range of shapes and motifs, most Sukhotai pieces are plates with underglaze black decoration, usually of fish. The free-form decoration is often more exuberant than on Sawankhalok ware. In excavations in southeast Asia, less than a quarter of the Thai ceramics that have been excavated come from Sukhotai. Production at Sukhotai died out before that at Sawankhalok, perhaps because the products were inferior to their rivals, or because the area was overwhelmed by the invading Burmese.

These two types are the most important Thai ceramics, both in terms of the scale of production and the quantity exported, though there were many other kiln sites and styles of ceramics. Look for Kalong ware mostly in celadon or in underglaze black, the latter often with animal motifs. The glaze is applied over a fine white body.

Vietnam

Annam, which means "the pacified south," was the name given to Vietnam by China. Although China dominated Vietnam for more than 1,000 years, it never managed to subjugate the people. "Annamese" is still used sometimes in connection with ceramics, but many people consider it colonial and, therefore, pejorative. In any case, Annam refers to only part of Vietnam. What is now central Vietnam was a separate kingdom called Champa. This region also produced brown-glazed ceramics that are now also called Vietnamese ware.

The Vietnamese, like the Thais, and often together with them, took advantage of the Chinese ban on independent trade at the beginning of the Ming period to develop their overseas markets. Once the Chinese reopened their foreign trade in the Qing dynasty, Vietnam's share of the southeast Asian market declined. In most excavations in southeast Asia, Vietnamese, Thai, and Chinese pieces are all found together.

In the past, people often labeled any unidentifiable piece of white ware with blue or black/brown underglaze decoration "Vietnamese." This is not an insult but a compliment to its quality, for the confusion exists only with regard to fine Chinese pieces. But it does the Vietnamese a disservice. They had almost as many centuries of experience as the Chinese in producing splendid ceramics of this type that stand very well on their own.

Champa ware has a body that turns pumpkin orange or bright pink when fired. Most other Vietnamese ware has a

Vietnamese beaker

grayish/white or buff body, spur marks in the center, and, sometimes, a chocolate brown wash on the base (Plate 19b). The reason for the brown wash is unknown: some writers suggest that it may designate pieces for temple use. Exports followed the same pattern of development as Chinese ceramics. Early pieces were mostly monochrome—brown, white, and celadon. Later, after the fifteenth century, came ceramics with underglaze blue decoration on a dirty white body.

Vietnamese ceramics have been excavated throughout southeast Asia, with the major concentrations in Indonesia. The largest collection is in Jakarta.

Kampuchea (Cambodia/Khmer)

The ceramic industry, which was concentrated mainly in the Angkor area, flourished for 400 years from the ninth century. Its products—mostly brown ware and some celadon—were not made for export. Yet a few pieces did reach southeast Asia, perhaps brought as tribute by ambassadors or carried by crew members. There have been only a few isolated finds, especially in Java and South Sumatra in Indonesia. Pieces have been found around the site of Majapahit, a flourishing royal city in the fourteenth and fifteenth centuries. Questionable pieces have been found around Butuan in the Philippines. Most pieces are on the Asian mainland, especially in Thailand where Khmer kilns were also located.

Though many Khmer pieces show Chinese and Indian influences, they have a style all their own. For a start, the parts that show are carefully made; the bases, on the other hand, are often sloppily finished. The decoration is geometrical, often with incised, straight, vertical lines. The very common brown-ware pots for domestic storage are much like Thai pots though they have a much more sculptural quality. Many have animal or bird heads, and tails or feet. The most appealing are undoubtedly the small pots for storing the lime used with betel nut. These are usually in the shape of birds and just ask to be held in the hand. So-called "honey pots" are very wide and very squat with a small hole in the top and a small flat handle in the shape of an animal. These brown wares usually have a thin, very dark glaze. It is the thinness of the glaze and its failure to bond with the biscuit that made Khmer pieces particularly subject to erosion during the time they were buried. Khmer potters also made some celadon ware.

Khmer pieces are available though not common. Some have been constructed from shards.

Korea

The Koryo dynasty (918–1392) was the first great age of Korean ceramics and celadon was its greatest product. Koryo ceramics were not exported except as tribute to foreign courts. As a result, they were almost unknown until

Koryo-dynasty covered box, Korea

early in the twentieth century, when many pieces were unearthed during construction of a railway by the Japanese. Uncontrolled excavation and grave robbing followed these first discoveries. The pieces showed Chinese influences, primarily from the Yue potters but also from later Song and Yuan potters. The Korean potters were much more than copyists. They were well-known and highly regarded. Koryo celadon was one of the "Eight Perfect Things Under Heaven," the Chinese said.

Korean celadon has a unique type of decoration. Fine inlays of colored clay make delicate, lacy designs and figures. Before the end of the twelfth century, Korean potters began using copper oxide to produce beautiful red colors. The Chinese did not use copper oxide as a pigment for painting under the glaze for at least another 100 years.

It was the imperfection and air of spontaneity that endeared Korean ceramics to the Japanese who prefered irregular shapes and glazes. Yi-dynasty (1392–1910) domestic ware, *punch'ong,* became all the rage in Japan after that country invaded Korea in 1592. What was everyday ware to Koreans became revered pieces to the Japanese, who coveted them for use in the tea ceremony. Naturally, this baffled the Koreans.

Antique Korean ceramics are not described extensively in this book.

Japan

Jomon earthenware pieces from about 10,000 BC are the earliest ceramics known. But because it had such a plentiful supply of wood for domestic use, Japan was a relative latecomer to the high-fired ceramic industry and its styles were adapted from those of China and Korea. Ceramics imported from the continent were used by the aristocracy and clergy and later by devotees of the tea ceremony. The Japanese fell in love with Chinese tea bowls, particularly those with dark or rough glazes and irregular shapes. They also adored Korean domestic *punch'ong* ware for use in the tea ceremony. In 1592 Japan invaded Korea and brought many potters back to Japan: estimates vary from hundreds to thousands of people. As well as making pottery in their own style, Korean émigré potters introduced Raku ware, straight-sided bowls perfectly suited to the Japanese taste for the imperfect. Under Korean tutelage and to meet the demands of the tea ceremony, ceramics became one of the supreme arts of Japan. Porcelain was not made in Japan until the Edo period.

Japanese ceramics are discussed only briefly in this book since Japan did not play much part in the major southeast Asian ceramic trade. Various styles are listed in **Talking Ceramics**. By the time the porcelain industry matured, much of its output was exported to Europe, although a good deal still went to southeast Asia. Blue-and-white ware with or without other colors was sold widely, largely by the Dutch East India Company.

Myanmar (Burma)

Except for the large, brown, glazed Martaban jars, little is known of the ceramics from this country. Recently pieces have been appearing from along the Thai/Myanmar border or from Myanmar itself—brown ware, celadons, bright greenwares, and white ware either plain or with green decoration.

THEMES AND
VARIATIONS

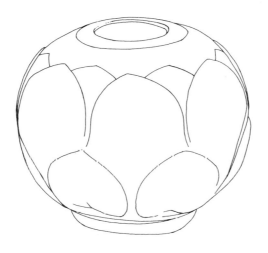

YUE WARE

The term Yue ware is used to describe ceramics produced during the Tang and Five Dynasties periods (the seventh to the tenth centuries), although it has a long tradition, starting as early as the fourth century. The very early ware is sometimes called "proto-Yue." The Chinese reserved the term Yue for superbly crafted green ware made in the principality of Wu Yue in northern Zhejiang province. Yue and Yue-type wares are often referred to as early green ware, that is, green ware of the seventh to tenth centuries. Examples of Yue ware have been discovered from Japan in the east to Egypt in the west.

Because of the high quality associated with the name, calling a piece "Yue" adds to its value, especially since very little true Yue ware went overseas. Often the export pieces are merely Yue in style. These pieces have a pale gray stoneware body; they are usually thinly potted, and well made. Most Yue jars and *kendi* appear to be made of sections joined together: there is often an angle or an incised line separating the various parts of a piece—neck, shoulders, and base. The footrim may be high and splayed; the base is usually glazed. These pieces have simple carved, stamped, or impressed decorations and a thin, dull gray-green, greenish-brown, or olive-greenish flaky glaze (Plate 19). Changsha ware, a green ware often having brown splashes on molded medallions, was made in Hunan province in the Tang and Five Dynasties period. It was heavily exported and is seen frequently today in southeast Asia (Plate 1).

Bowls "like dewy, budding lotus flowers" imitated gold and silver pieces of the period. Yue pieces in the "secret color," a misty olive green, were reserved for the Wu Yue royal family and for tribute to their Song overlords.

GREEN WARE / CELADON

History

Green ware and celadon are synonymous except for bright green pieces that are lead-glazed (Plate 5). (*See* the **Lead-Glazed Ware** section below.) The name celadon is a Western, not an Asian name. Yet celadon was never produced outside Asia. People named the color after Celadon, a character in a seventeenth-century French play who wore a greenish costume. At least, that is what the *Oxford Dictionary* says. Other sources report that the name means "sheathed in jade" or refers to Saladin, the Sultan of Egypt, who in 1171 sent some pieces of it as a gift to another sultan. The glaze appears to float above the surface of the piece (Plate 11). However, if the glazing and the firing conditions are not quite right, the pieces may be gold, green, olive, brown, turquoise, or blue and may lack sheen (Plates 6, 7, 13).

Potters make celadon by adding a small amount of iron oxide to the glaze mixture. Then they fire the piece at a high temperature, being careful to allow very little air into the kiln. This is called firing in a reducing atmosphere. The amount of air that enters the kiln largely determines the color. Little air—green; more air—green to yellow to turquoise to gray. To collectors, celadons represent the old aristocracy of ceramics.

Production of Yue ware declined in the Northern Song period. But production of celadon ware continued in the Longquan (Lung-ch'üan) area, which is also in Zhejiang province. As demand for green ware grew, hundreds of kilns in the southern part of Zhejiang province became active.

Celadon ware reached its artistic and technical pinnacle during the Southern Song era. In fact, some experts argue that Song celadon is the supreme accomplishment of the potter's craft. The most highly prized Song celadon comes mainly from the Longquan group. These wares were popular, attractive, and of a high quality that was maintained through to Ming times. Other green wares of lesser quality were being produced simultaneously with Longquan ware in Fujian, at Xicun and Chaoan in Guangdong, and in other provinces of south China. Here again the words "green ware" can be a trap. These pieces are not all green. They may be gold, grayish, or olive.

Celadons were shipped from China from the Northern Song era into the Ming period. Some true Longquan ware found its way to southeast Asia but most pieces were good imitations from kilns in other parts of China. In the Yuan period, much celadon was designed to be produced en masse for the export market. From 1350 to 1500, huge quantities of celadon also came from the Sawankhalok kilns in Thailand. Even when blue-and-white ware came to dominate the export market, celadon continued to be popular in the export trade, especially celadon from the Longquan kilns.

Vietnam did not export much celadon ware. After the fourteenth century, celadon appears to have been discontinued in favor of apple-green glaze.

Korean celadon of the Koryo period is similar to Chinese Song, but is quieter. One writer says that it "waits for you."

Both Korean and Thai potters are making beautiful celadon ware today. Korean ware is a lighter, bluer color. Ming Rai pieces made in Thailand are especially fine and can be mistaken for fifteenth-century pieces.

Appearance

Shape

The Song potters achieved a wonderful simplicity of form. The pieces just ask to be handled. Shapes copied from ancient bronze vessels such as jars and bowls became fashionable, particularly in Southern Song. These are sometimes described as handsome, rather than pretty. More mundane pieces were also plentiful.

By this period, it is difficult to identify a piece just by shape. Thai potters had much the same repertoire for export ware as the Chinese. Especially during the fourteenth century, the output from both countries was varied and enormous. Plates, saucers, bowls, jugs, jars, jarlets, and covered jars were most common. Both the Chinese and the Thai also made dishes as large as 50 cm in diameter. These often had foliated or scalloped rims to disguise warping or

Celadon jarlets. Stoneware. China. Song period. 6 cm high.

sagging edges. Both the Thai and the Chinese also made celadon jars 12 cm high with handles. The Thai pieces usually have incised horizontal lines on the shoulders and handles placed vertically like ears (Plate 7); Chinese jars generally have no lines and the handles are horizontal. They are all called "Grenadas" in the Philippines because they are the same shape as hand grenades.

Changsha pieces are most likely to be small figurines or late Tang ewers with short, straight spouts, and handles like straps (Plate 1).

Korean potters also made a wide range of ceramics and were as adept as the Chinese at making large jars. Many pieces had lobes.

Glaze

In Northern Song-period ware, the glazes tend toward light green with a touch of olive; they have little crackle. The Southern Song potters who followed achieved a beautiful color—a clear, soft, translucent green with a bluish tone.

Celadon jar called a Grenada. Stoneware. The two earlike handles and incised lines are characteristic of Sawankhalok jars. Sawankhalok, Thailand. 10 cm high.

They relied for appeal partly on shape. But they counted most on beautiful glazes, which are thick and often have an obvious crackle.Yuan glazes tend to be greener than Song (Plate 11). People prize Southern Song celadon the most highly of all green ware (Plate 12).

The traditions of the Song period continued into the Yuan period. In the Ming era, the glazes tended to be thinner and to lack the lustre of earlier pieces (Plate 13).

Thai potters could not duplicate the creamy feel and rich lively greens of the best Chinese celadons. They used less opaque glazes, which they applied thinly. They were not as concerned as the Chinese about hiding the elemental qualities of clay. They also had more trouble controlling the air flow in their kilns. As a result, the green is usually paler than on Chinese pieces, and the colors range through tan to deep olive to gray-green to grayish blue to turquoise. The last color is especially attractive.

In some pieces from all these countries, the glaze does not extend to the base. This is because the potter was afraid the glazes might run down unevenly and fuse the pot to the kiln support.

On Korean celadons, the glazes are generally thinner and not as carefully applied as on Chinese pieces.

Potting

Much Song ware is light in weight, but what was exported was generally heavier because it was less likely to break in transit. In the Yuan period, the pieces became larger and the potting heavier. These trends continued into the Ming period.

Sawankhalok celadon dishes and bowls are similar to but heavier than Vietnamese and Song and Yuan Chinese pieces. Other shapes of Sawankhalok celadon tend to be about the same weight as their Vietnamese and Chinese counterparts.

Base / Footrim

The clay showing on the base of Northern Song ware is often brown to dark gray. (*See* **Watch the Bottom Line.**) On Southern Song ware, the exposed footrims show light gray to white clay; sometimes the firing turned the base terra-cotta red, which does not happen on Northern Song ware. Guangdong ware has white or grayish-white clay.

On Northern Song pieces, the bases usually are unglazed. Earlier, Yue or Yue-type wares have glazed bases. On the best Southern Song pieces, the bases are glazed, but inferior pieces have unglazed bases. Unglazed bases are most common in southeast Asia. Despite the perfection of the upper part, the base of many pieces is roughly finished. This rough finish continued into the Yuan period. Jarlets of the later period are usually unglazed around the entire base. However, some pieces are well finished and cleanly glazed.

Chinese celadons of the Yuan and Ming dynasties can often be recognized by an unglazed reddish base, or an unglazed reddish ring on the base (Plate 13b).

Sawankhalok wares have minute black particles in the gray/beige clay, which may turn a reddish color when fired.

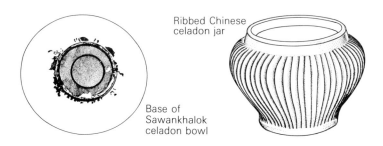

Base of Sawankhalok celadon bowl

Ribbed Chinese celadon jar

Frequently, the base has a dark ring, or the vestiges of a ring, where the piece rested on the lighthouse kiln support. Inside the ring, the clay may still be grey (Plate 6).

Korean celadons often have little lumps like sesame seeds on the base. These came from the stand on which the piece stood during firing.

Decoration

Changsha pieces have molded medallions with splashes of brown glaze on them (Plate 1).

Northern Song celadons were decorated by molding, stamping, incising, combing, and carving. Lotus buds, flowers, and leaves are the most common forms. Fish, ducks, and butterflies appeared later, often together with wave-like carvings. Some incised floral designs are elaborate, covering the whole piece.

Southern Song ware generally has less decoration than Northern Song. The court was run by scholars who preferred sophisticated, elegant pieces in one color. Most often the designs are simple, leaving most of the body plain. Where there is decoration, the same motifs as on Northern Song ware are incised. Precise ribbing and fluting and molded decoration are common.

In the Yuan period, quality remained high but potters stamped and applied much more decoration, choosing from a much wider range of motifs. They found it much faster to use a carved mold, or to apply pre-molded decoration to a finished piece, than to carve each piece individually. The pair of fish symbolizing marital bliss, which is so often found on celadon plates, or the rarer single carp, are examples of applied work. Only on celadon pieces of this period are unglazed fish and other relief decoration found. Other oddities include pieces with iron brown spots used for decoration or to disguise inferior potting.

In the Ming period, the traditional celadon motifs—phoenixes, dragons, peonies, and chrysanthemums—were still incised and molded. The glazes were still applied richly.

In Sawankhalok pieces, simple geometric and floral designs are often incised under the glaze (Plate 10). Though the Thais did not try to copy Chinese designs precisely, they incised peonies, lotus buds, scroll patterns, ribbing, and fluting like lotus petals—all Chinese motifs. Often these were applied in a freer style than on Chinese pieces. The flutes on the outside may be less regular and the flowers incised in the center of the inside less formal. Some superb pieces, however, match the formality and precision of the best from China (Plates 11, 12).

At first Korean celadons were incised, molded, or plain. By the mid-twelfth century, potters had developed a distinctive inlay technique, carving out delicate designs that they filled in with black and white or colored slip. Flowers were the most commonly used designs.

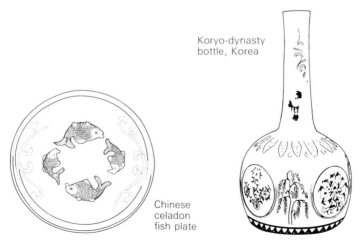

Koryo-dynasty
bottle, Korea

Chinese
celadon
fish plate

BROWN WARE

History

Ceramics with a brown glaze are hard to categorize. People assume that most pieces found in southeast Asia are Chinese and were made for several centuries beginning in the Song period. Some, indeed, are Song: we know that many pieces were made in Guangdong and Fujian provinces in the thirteenth and fourteenth centuries. But many others could just as easily be from Thailand or Vietnam. This uncertainty may be one of the reason scholars and buyers have paid less attention to brown ware than to celadon or blue-and-white. Or perhaps they have simply found brown ware less elegant, too simple. But its very simplicity is its charm (Plates 2–4).

The Khmer ware of Kampuchea is described at the end of the **Ages and Origins** chapter.

Appearance

Shape

Plates and bowls for tea or rice are often seen; jars abound. Jars were exported in huge quantities, sometimes packed inside even larger ones. They range from items useful in small kitchens to huge models for storing water or for burial.

At the small end of brown ware come flared bowls from China, and jarlets, vases, bowls, figurines, and covered boxes from Thailand. Commonly found are Sawankhalok pots with three vertical handles and domed lids with knobs on the top (Plate 3). Vietnamese potters made beakers, bowls, plates, jarlets, and ewers.

The next size up are *kendi,* and narrow, tapered jars, usually about 12 cm high. These jars, made by both the Chinese and the Thai, are shaped like hand grenades. They were also made in celadon (Plate 7). Jars with vertical ears are especially, although not uniquely, characteristic of Sawankhalok. Vertical ears are also found on Chinese pieces, but horizontal loops seem more common. After strings were run through the holes, the jugs could be filled with oil or condiments and hung out of reach of predators.

Pots 15 to 30 cm high form a big group. They usually have loops on the shoulders and wider bodies and mouths than the grenade-shaped jars. They are likely Song in period, from south China, possibly from Guangdong or Fujian provinces. About the same size are well proportioned, simple vases with flared lips, short necks, and rounded bodies from Vietnam.

Large jars from 40 to 60 cm high form a further category. They were made in all three countries. Most jars are plain except for their handles. Large decorated water jars thought to be Chinese are known as Martaban jars, after the port in Burma from which they were shipped. They were made from the Song to the Qing dynasties for carrying food, oil,

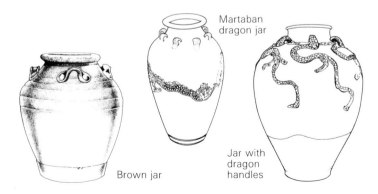

Martaban
dragon jar

Brown jar

Jar with
dragon
handles

or water. The mouths are small and near the top of the shoulders are as many as eight horizontal handles. Thai pots come in the same sizes but are more bulbous than any of the other styles. Indonesian buyers thought the large jars were magical, that they fell down from the sky. They took such good care of them that examples are still common.

Body

The paste of Chinese brown ware is usually gray to white except for the famous Jian bowls of Fujian province, which are made from very dark, coarse clay. Much of this ware is known as *temmoku* ware, the name given it by the Japanese who adopted the style with great enthusiasm. (Some pieces from Hebei and Honan look like *temmoku* ware and are given that name, but have light-colored bodies.) Thai pieces have a buff body that often fired reddish. The body of much Vietnamese brown ware is likely the usual grayish/white/buff. Champa wares have a bright pink or pumpkin orange body from the iron in the clay.

Glaze

On many pieces, from all three countries, the thin glaze has flaked off, eroded, or worn away, especially around the rims and handle edges. The glazes may be thin dark brown, light brown, golden brown, or olive brown. The glazes must have been very runny. Often they do not come even part way down the vessel, let alone close to the bottom (Plate 4).

A less common Chinese style is the Jian ware, *temmoku*-type, tea bowl. This distinctive piece has a dark brown shiny glaze that forms into a roll just above the foot where the bowl is angled to prevent the glaze from dripping down to the base. Sometimes these pieces, especially bowls about 8 cm across, have hare's-fur markings (Plate 2). Jian ware may also have an almost transparent yellow-brown glaze.

Occasionally the glaze on Jizhou pieces shows streaks, marks, or patches of other colors—blue, black, or silver. Often the glaze has a mottled appearance caused, it is suspected, in the firing when the intended brown partly turned to olive.

Martaban jars have a golden brown glaze, usually with a nice rich sheen. It too ends above the base. A thick, warm brown or dark, rich brown glaze, often with bubbles, is found on some very small and very large Sawankhalok jars. The glaze does not come to the base.

Vietnamese ware often has a dark brown glaze, but comes in other shades of brown as well. Champa wares have a caramel-color glaze that stops short of the base.

Base / Footrim

The base of jars is almost flat or only slightly concave. The base of bowls and pots is usually square cut. Bases are generally not glazed. Footrims may be glazed occasionally. On Jian ware, the base is unglazed and sometimes does not rest flat.

Decoration

Small and medium-sized Chinese jars are usually plain. Small boxes with molded, clear-glazed medallions on the top and a brown glaze on the rest of the body are Yuan period, from southern China. Large jars from Guangdong and Fujian may have incised patterns, such as markings that imitate the surface of a pineapple. Many Martaban jars have raised, flying dragons.

Thai brown wares have horizontal incised circles around the shoulders and on the lids of covered pieces (Plate 3). On some pieces, incised grooves run vertically. Vietnamese brown ware is either plain or has incised free-form leaves, flowers, and curving lines.

Plate 1
Changsha jug with loop handles. 3 molded plaques with brown glaze over them. China. Tang dynasty. 17 cm high.

Plate 2
Jian hare's-fur bowl. China. Song or Yuan dynasties. 11.5 cm across.

Plate 3
Covered jar with domed top, three ears, and concentric incised circles. Stoneware. The brown glaze is thin on the handles and the edges. The glaze does not extend to the foot-rim. The clay, which turned reddish when fired, has black flecks. Sawankhalok, Thailand. 10 cm high.

Plate 4
Brown jar with four handles. The thin glaze, which does not go to the base, is eroded around the neck, lip, and handles. The body is gray/beige stoneware. Possibly from Guangdong, China. Song dynasty. 16 cm high.

Plate 5
Pouring vessel in the form of two ducks. One duck is predominantly lead-glazed. The color sits on the surface: it does not seem to emanate from within the piece. China. Ming dynasty. 13 cm high.

Plate 6
Shard of a celadon bowl.
Stoneware. The glaze
has pooled above the
footrim. The thick base is
red outside and gray
inside the dark ring made
by the kiln support.
Sawankhalok, Thailand.
15th century.

Plate 7
Celadon jar. Stoneware.
Soft blue-green glaze.
The two earlike handles
and incised lines are characteristic of Sawankhalok
jars. This glaze is pleasant but not as rich as
many Chinese glazes.
Similar jars were made
with a brown glaze.
Sawankhalok, Thailand.
10 cm high.

Plate 8
Small celadon bowl with thin, shiny, beige-green glaze. Combing and incising. Clay is gray. Footrim is glazed. China. Northern Song. 10 cm across. (See *base* in Watch the Bottom Line.)

Plate 9
Green-ware bowl with octopus foliation and roughly incised flowers. Bronze-green dull glaze. Clay is light gray. China, Fujian or Guangdong provinces. Yuan dynasty. 19 cm across.

Plate 10
Green-ware dish with glassy-green glaze. Stoneware with crackled glaze. Incised decoration. Sawankhalok, Thailand. 28 cm across.

Plate 11
Covered box with molded floral spray. Thick, smooth, gray-green glaze.
Stoneware. China. Yuan dynasty. 9 cm across.

Plate 12
Lotus bowl. Carved decoration on the outside with radiating lotus petals
on the cover. Gray stoneware with blue-green glaze. China, Longquan
ware. Song dynasty. 8 cm high.

Plate 13a
Celadon saucer with eight sides. Stoneware. Lines and swirls are incised around the flat edge. The middle has an impressed lotus flower. China. Ming dynasty. 17 cm wide.

Plate 13b
The footrim of the saucer is glazed; the base is unglazed; the clay body is reddish.

Plate 14a
Dehua saucer, white, with two impressed fish. Porcelain. The fish are skeletal. The light gray clay is chalky. Unglazed inner rim. Fujian province, China. Yuan dynasty. 14 cm across.

Plate 14b
The footrim of the Dehua saucer is short and not cleanly cut or finished. The glaze is unevenly applied. Base and footrim are unglazed.

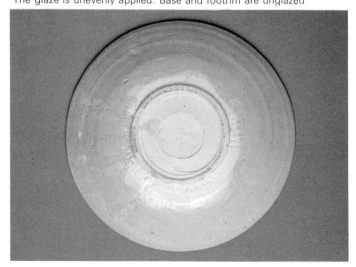

Plate 15a
Qingbai saucer with incised and combed lotus blossom in the center.
Porcelain. The misty blue glaze is on a thin, delicate body. China. Yuan
dynasty. 17 cm across.

Plate 15b
The footrim of this *qingbai* saucer is thinly glazed. On the whitish clay of
the unglazed base, some brown clay still clings from the pontil.

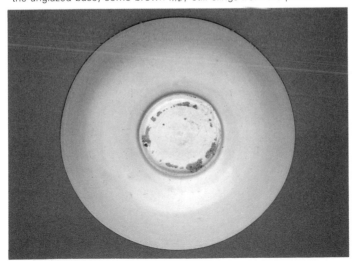

Plate 16
Covered boxes in the shape of reliquary urns. Stoneware. The underglaze black decoration is roughly applied. The patterns flow from the upper to the lower sections. A brownish glaze has been applied around the lotus handles on the lids and on the slanted footrims. This is typical of many Sawankhalok boxes. The clay bodies are pinkish/beige with black flecks. The bases are unglazed. Sawankhalok, Thailand. 11 and 9 cm high.

Plate 17
Bowl with design of fish bones and eyes. Stoneware. Beige/gray clay, unglazed base. Yue-type ware. China. Song dynasty. 10 cm high.

Plate 18
Bowl. Cream-white stoneware with thin chocolate exterior glaze. A ring of glaze was cut away on the bottom before firing so that the pieces would not stick together when stacked in the kiln. Glaze stops above the footrim. Vietnam. 14–15th century. 18 cm across.

Plates 19a, 19b
Vietnamese dish decorated in underglaze blue. Bird on a flowering
branch surrounded by complex design of stylized waves, flowers, and
scrolling leaf sprays and bands. The base shows the distinctive brown
wash or "chocolate base" that identifies much Vietnamese ware.
15–16th century. 36.5 cm across.

Plate 20
Covered box with blue-and-white underglaze painting. Stoneware. Geometric panels are typical. Sides and top are decorated as one. The well-finished footrim is unglazed. Vietnam. 15–16th century. 5 cm high.

Plate 21
Blue-and-white bowl with dragon. Porcelain. The painting is clear and precise. The body is white with no tinge of blue. The glazed base and footrim are well finished. China. Qing dynasty. 23 cm across.

Plates 22a, 22b
Plate with blue-and-white floral decoration. White porcelain with a milky glaze with a blue-green tint. The painting of abstract floral motifs, in several shades of blue, was energetically but quickly applied. Unglazed line in interior bottom. Called Canton ware, Kitchen Qing, and Hong Kong, Shanghai, or Singapore ware. The outside of the plate has the usual simple lines around the cavetto. The base is glazed, with cursive script. China. Ming dynasty. 31 cm across.

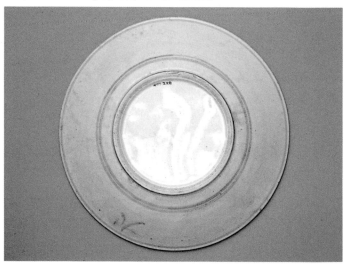

Plates 23a, 23b
Shantou (Swatow) dish decorated in overglaze enamels. Turquoise fish leaping from green waves alternate with stylized lotus bouquets and water grasses in red and green. Note the lack of decoration on the underside and the rough finish on the base. China. Ming dynasty. 37 cm across.

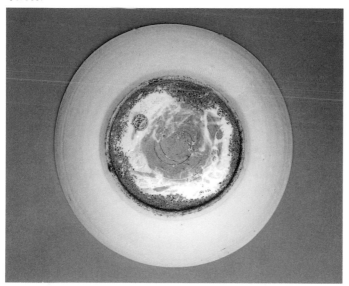

Plate 24
Vase with long, slender neck. White porcelain with lustrous red glaze.
No decoration. China. Qing dynasty. 22 cm high.

LEAD-GLAZED WARE

Tang colors, bright green and amber, reappeared in China on ceramics that were likely made in Fujian province from the Song through to the Ming periods. The colors were made by adding copper to the lead glaze for green, and iron for amber. The glaze is clearly on the surface and does not seem to emanate from inside the piece itself, the way many celadon glazes do. Pieces may have only one color or may have amber and green combined. Most were not carefully made; they may be crooked, unevenly glazed, or ave messy bases. The clay is generally white (Plate 5).

Chinese lead-glazed ware is found throughout southeast Asia. The most common shapes are small pots, teapots, jarlets, water droppers, figurines, and *kendi*. Some large jars 50 cm high have been recovered.

In the thirteenth and fourteenth centuries, Vietnamese potters produced saucers, bowls, and covered boxes with a lively apple-green glaze, thinly applied. Many pieces were exported. The dishes sometimes have unglazed center rings: most pieces have unglazed carved feet. Many have the characteristic chocolate wash on the base.

Lead-glazed jar. Perhaps from Fujian province. Song dynasty. 10 cm high.

UNDERGLAZE BLACK/BROWN WARE

History

A fascinatingly varied class of Oriental ceramics has black or brown decoration with a clear glaze applied over it to protect the pattern. In shape and design these pieces are just as lively as the more famous blue-and-white wares. They were also made in all three major ceramic-producing countries—China, Vietnam, and Thailand—whereas blue-and-white ware was made only in the first two.

The popular Cizhou (Tz'u-chou) ware was made in northern China from the tenth to the fourteenth centuries. These kilns were among the first in that country to have black/brown decoration painted over a white slip and under a clear glaze. Cizhou had the widest range of decoration of any Chinese ware. Jizhou ware from Jiangxi province was made around the same period. One variety of the ware shows the influence of Cizhou techniques in its use of dark underglaze painting on slip. The names sound so alike that the styles are frequently confused.

Design on a Cizhou
covered jar

Another famous style, Changsha ware, was made in Hunan province in the Tang and Five Dynasties periods. It is described in the Yue/green ware chapter. Other Chinese underglaze black/brown pieces likely came from Xicun or other kilns in Guangdong, or from Jian in Fujian province. Some Chinese pieces look as though they have underglaze black decoration, but it is really blue-and-white gone wrong.

Sawankhalok pieces in this style have a character all their own. They show Chinese influences and often come close to matching Chinese quality, though they are not as delicate, symmetrical, or perfect. Sukhotai pieces are even more recognizable. The potting is rough; some pieces are mis-shapen and crude, but the decoration is free and attractive.

Although Vietnamese potters also kept their originality, their work shows that everyone in the potting business in southeast Asia knew what the competition was doing. Vietnamese covered boxes look like Sawankhalok, Cizhou, and Jizhou pieces, and Vietnamese underglaze black/brown painting has an uncanny resemblance to Sukhotai decoration. From the fourteenth century on, the most common Vietnamese export pieces were underglaze black.

Appearance

Shape

The most common shapes of Cizhou ware are bowls and *guan*-shaped jars in a wide variety of sizes, often very large and boldly executed. Jizhou pieces are usually small tea bowls, jars, and vases.

What most people call jars or pots with lids are called, in ceramic terminology, covered boxes. They are characteristic of Sawankhalok ware and are among the finest and most common pieces from that area (Plate 16). They were used for storing food, spices, medicines, cosmetics, etc. Sizes range from 5 to 18 cm high. Boxes come in two main styles. One is fruit shaped, like a mangosteen or persimmon. The other looks like a reliquary urn with a lid handle in the shape of a small lotus (Plate 16). A third, less common style, has six to eight facets.

Sawankhalok potters also made plates, bowls, *kendi,* small pots, vases with long necks and squat bodies, ewers, lamps, and figurines and animals with black/brown underglaze decoration. The best Sawankhalok animals have sloping backs and rosettes on their cheeks. From the Sukhotai kilns came plates, bowls, jars, and pear-shaped bottles. Plates are most common.

Bowls and dishes, covered boxes, and water droppers are the most commonly found underglaze black pieces from Vietnam.

Clay

Most Cizhou and Jizhou ware has a buff or light gray body. Most Chinese ware in this category has grayish clay.

The clay used in Sawankhalok pieces is slightly coarse. It is easy to identify because it has minute black particles. Sawankhalok shards will likely be medium gray inside and brown to reddish on the exposed surfaces (Plate 6). In Sukhotai ware, the brown clay is thick and grainier than Sawankhalok ware, and has white particles.

Vietnamese stoneware comes in white, grayish white, or buff. It is smooth and dense with few impurities (Plate 18).

Potting

Sawankhalok underglaze black pieces are more finely potted than Sawankhalok celadons. The walls are comparatively thin. The casual manner of the Sukhotai potters carried over into the potting and firing, unfortunately. Many pieces are warped or sagging.

Vietnamese pieces are often better potted and glazed although they may be a bit heavier.

Glaze

Cizhou ware usually has slip and a transparent glaze, lead glaze, or overglaze enameling. Jizhou ware, on the other hand, often has painting using pale slip on a dark ground or the reverse, or two layers of glazing that looks like tortoise shell. The rest of the body has a clear glaze. Most other Chinese pieces with underglaze black or brown painting have clear glazes.

The glaze on Sawankhalok pieces is transparent or grayish, though where it gathers in a puddle it has a milky-blue tinge. Because the clay was fine, the potters did not need to apply slip. The inside of Sawankhalok boxes is glazed, but not the lid. Often the topknot on the lid, a bit of the clay around it, and the footrim are brown, no matter the color of the rest of the piece (Plate 16). Sometimes the clear glaze looks yellowy-greenish when it pools, just like Sukhotai and Vietnamese ware. One museum describes the milky glaze on the covered boxes as having an "opalescent cloudiness."

On Sukhotai pieces, thick, white slip covers only part of the body. Glazes are thin, almost transparent, and have a yellow, blue, or green tinge. Often the glaze did not fuse with the clay. It may be full of tiny holes and may flake off easily. Some wares were left unglazed and some have unglazed rims.

Vietnamese potters needed only a clear glaze over their painted decoration since their clay was so white and fine. Some pieces have crackle and may look almost opaque.

Base / Footrim

It is not possible to generalize about footrims on Cizhou pieces. On most Jizhou, the glaze stops above the footrim.

On Sawankhalok pieces, the footrim is clean. It may show the trademark brown ring or remnants of a ring on the base where the piece was fastened to the lighthouse support (Plate 6). Most Sukhotai bowls and plates have five small circular spur marks on the inside bottom. These were made by the supports used to separate each piece during firing. Occasionally the base will have a round mark from a tubular support. The base is always unglazed. The footrim is big and rough.

It is almost impossible to generalize about the shapes, rims, and feet of Vietnamese pieces. Sometimes there are five or six spur marks or an unglazed center ring on the interior of black-and-white pieces. The spur marks on early Vietnamese ware tend to be almost triangular. The Sukhotai marks are round. The surest sign of a Vietnamese piece, when you can find it, is the mysterious chocolate wash on the base.

Decoration

Cizhou decorations include bold animals, phoenixes, and flowers painted in black. Sometimes they are incised, with cuts made straight down through the glaze and slip. (In contrast, celadon, for example, was usually incised with the tool held at an angle.) Jizhou potters used brown painting on a cream ground and slip painting on backgrounds of various shades of brown as well as black.

Sawankhalok boxes usually have restrained underglaze black decorations in leaf, scroll, and geometric designs very much in the Cizhou style. The design on the top forms a whole with the design on the base (Plate 16). The same patterns are also found on Vietnamese ware. Many

Sawankhalok pieces show Indian influences: these are decorated with repeated patterns reminiscent of Indian printed fabrics. *Kendi* are often decorated with motifs from local temple reliefs. Unique to Sawankhalok are incised designs, which often combine sawtooth patterns and scrolly, vegetal patterns. Sometimes the design is brown on an ivory/pearl ground; other times, the colors are reversed. Some covered boxes are plain white except for the lid, which may have an incised floral design covered with brown glaze.

The decoration on many Sukhotai and Vietnamese pieces resembles some Cizhou ware—freestyle brushstrokes and plenty of clear background. Both may have a sketchy

Incised Sawankhalok bottle

Sawankhalok covered box

freeform central flower and a scrolly calligraphic border. Many Vietnamese bowls have simple floral sprays in the center and casual curves and lines on the rim: they look very much like Sukhotai ware. On the plain background, the glaze is often crackled.

Almost all Sukhotai ware is decorated with underglaze black painting of fish, whirling discs, tiered crowns, scrolling tendrils, or floral sprays on medallions. Sukhotai pieces have humor and freedom. The potters who painted the big, freeform fish obviously had fun. Often the fish seem to be grinning. A rare piece, a bowl found in Butuan, the Philippines, has a black speckled bird and a fish. Fish plates are much sought after.

Vietnamese potters mostly made simple pieces. However, they also made elaborate pieces with formal, all-over floral designs.

Vietnamese underglaze black saucer with central flower

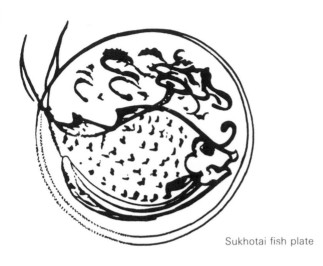

Sukhotai fish plate

Sukhotai plate with
whirling disc pattern

WHITE AND ALMOST WHITE WARE

History

The search for the perfect pure white ceramic body preoccupied potters for centuries. Since the Tang era, Chinese potters had made many beautiful styles of high-fired white ware using just one type of clay. In the early fourteenth century, they mixed several clays to produce porcelain, a thin, white, hard, smooth ceramic that needs only a clear glaze. Success was first achieved in Jiangxi province at the Jingdezhen kilns.

One of the most beautiful of the plain glazed ceramics is *qingbai*, a white ceramic with a misty blue tinge to the glaze (Plate 15). It was produced for three centuries, well into the Yuan period, in Fujian, Guangdong, and Jiangxi provinces. The largest center of *qingbai* production was at Jingdezhen.

Qingbai was exported in large quantities. A variety, *qingbai* with brown iron spots, was made mostly for the export market. Even though spotted pieces are always small and often not well made, they have a definite charm. It is not difficult to find pleasant Yuan pieces. Good pieces, however, are rare and much prized. Very few spotted ceramics have been found in China itself.

Another important Chinese white ware from Jingdezhen is Shufu ware, which was also produced during the Yuan period. Some pieces have two inscribed characters, Shu and Fu, meaning Privy Council. It is supposed that the best quality pieces were made for the Yuan Imperial household. Wasters were exported. *Qingbai* and Shufu wares set the stage for blue-and-white ware, since they provided the ideal base for blue decoration.

The Dehua kilns were in Fujian province. They produced white porcelain, blue-and-white, and *qingbai* from the Song to the Qing dynasties (Plates 14a, 14b). Their work is well represented in southeast Asia. Dehua is also called Marco Polo ware because that great traveler is reputed to have taken a piece back to Venice. Starting in the sixteenth century, Dehua produced a white, smooth porcelain called *blanc de chine*. When they are in good condition, the pieces look as if they were made yesterday.

Between the lightness of *qingbai* and the solidity of Shufu, there is a range of white ware that can be described only in the most general terms. While *qingbai* can be from many provinces and has a distinct appearance, and Dehua is from Fujian and Shufu from Jingdezhen, many other white pieces defy such precise identification. Occasional pieces may be called Jingdezhen, but mostly the kiln sites are just starting to be explored. These pieces can be called after their provincial source if it is known. Some other experts prefer to group them all together under the heading "transitional" white ware, the transition being from the elegance and simplicity of Song ware to the molded decoration and blue underglaze painting of the late Yuan period.

Both Thailand and Vietnam produced white ware. Vietnam made more white ware than green or brown ware. A wide range of white ware—as wide as the Chinese range—was produced until the sixteenth century.

Appearance

Shape

The shapes of many white-ware pieces, especially bowls, changed in the eleventh and twelfth centuries, although the refined, simple forms of the Song period carried over into the Yuan age. Mass production demanded quick, simple techniques. Flared rather than rounded shapes became more common, as it is easier to press clay onto a mold with straight sides than onto a rounded mold.

Qingbai pieces come in many shapes—small bowls, saucers, plates, and small vessels. Many of the early shapes imitate lacquerware. While it is rare to find *qingbai* boxes in China, they are not uncommon in southeast Asia. Figurines have become more difficult to find. The most appealing and most common spotted pieces are *balimbing* jarlets, and single or double gourd pots with spouts. It is almost impossible to find a gourd pot with a spout that has not been repaired or replaced.

Dehua, Shufu, and other Chinese white or grayish-white wares common in southeast Asia are plates, covered boxes, bowls, and vases. Countless small pieces have also been found—jars and jarlets mainly. These often have round or oval shapes, little loop handles at the neck, and are fluted or beaded or both. The most common characteristic of these pieces is that they are not trimmed to make them smooth and symmetrical. They have a very rough appearance, especially around the base. Less common are pots shaped like baskets with rounded bottoms and vertical bands constricting the top. Production of many common shapes continued into the Ming period—plain bowls, lotus-shaped bowls, stem bowls, and dishes.

Yuan flared stem cup

Notable export pieces of *blanc de chine* are small, very detailed, curving figures, and statues of Buddha and Guanyin; the most common exports were small containers.

Sawankhalok white ware includes vases with cup-shaped mouths; deep, rounded bowls; and covered pots, some with vertical handles and some with no handles. These same shapes are often found with brown glaze also.

Clay / Potting

It is hard to distinguish pieces from the different Chinese provinces. *Qingbai* ware generally is famous for its fine potting. The pieces are thin and delicate but strong. The clay is chalky white: the unglazed portion may be white or have turned pinkish during firing. Many other pieces from Guangdong province share these characteristics, but have a clear glaze without the bluish color distinctive to true *qingbai*.

The fine-grained, white, porcelain body of Shufu pieces is thicker and heavier than *qingbai*. The clay used at Dehua is chalky, and the pieces are of medium thickness, which makes it easy to tell them from *qingbai*. Other pieces from Fujian are made of the same chalky clay.

In Sawankhalok pieces, the clay can be gray or off-white, and the biscuit may be tinged with pink. Vietnamese pieces have the usual white or buff clay, which is very smooth and fine. It is often difficult to distinguish between Chinese porcelain and Vietnamese white ware.

Glaze

Qingbai is written with the two characters *qing,* which means either green or blue, and *bai,* which means white. *Yingqing,* which means lustrous jade green, is an alternate name. The almost white pieces are known for their translucency and for the transparency and glossiness of their glazes. They sometimes have a slight yellowish tinge. Often the footrim is unglazed because the pieces were fired upside down.

In contrast, Shufu ware has a milky, opaque, thick matt glaze, which is equally recognizable. The grayish-white glaze of Dehua's white ware is opaque, looks dense like putty, and is less glowing than *qingbai* (Plates 14a–15b). Superior pieces have a warmer color and a better finish. By the sixteenth century, Dehua had started to produce the pure white porcelain known as *blanc de chine*.

Early Ming white ware tended to have a glaze with very fine pits. Later the glaze became smooth. Since the shapes are like those of earlier periods, the glaze helps determine the age.

On Sawankhalok white ware, the glazes are thin and pebbly, sometimes with a blue tinge. Some pieces have a pearly look. Others are crackled. Some Vietnamese pieces have a very smooth glaze.

Base / Footrim

If the rims are unglazed because the piece was fired upside down, the footrim will be glazed. The foot of many *qingbai* pieces is thin and low with a roughly cut base, often unglazed (Plate 15b). Early Jingdezhen *qingbai* bowls often have strong, high feet. Shufu footrims may be thick and square. On bowls, the foot is usually flared. The base of Shufu pieces is often unglazed. Sometimes it has a little nipple at the center and a burnt orange tone. Sometimes there is almost no foot. Dehua white wares have thin footrims and are roughly finished (Plate 14b).

On the white pieces known now by province alone, the feet are generally thin and not too well formed and finished. Most often the bases and footrims are unglazed. In the Yuan period, the white ware becomes somewhat heavier and the bases are quite rough.

Sawankhalok pots and bowls generally have straight or slightly flared cut footrims. The base often has the characteristic full or partial brown ring where the piece rested on the pontil during firing (Plate 6). Vietnamese pieces may have an unglazed ring (Plate 18) or spur marks inside, have an unglazed rim, be glazed all over, or have an unglazed or brown washed base. The only common feature is that the feet are usually neatly cut and finished.

Decoration

The elegant, refined decorative techniques of *qingbai* ware include combing and light incising (Plate 15). Dotted combing is also found: the comb appears to have been poked at an angle into the clay, making rows of short marks. During the Yuan period the combing and incising became heavier, and beading, like that often found on Buddhist sculpture, became common. Sometimes the rim is banded in silver or copper, or has small lobes. Sometimes one flower, a fully opened lotus, for example, will be carved in the center. Molding became important in Southern Song pieces which are often molded inside, and occasionally outside

Beaded *qingbai* jarlet

Sometimes they have a molded sunburst design. Often the molding is divided into panels.

Spotted *qingbai* pieces are from the Yuan period. The brown spots were made with iron. They may have been applied to divert the eye from inferior potting or simply for decoration. The technique was introduced on proto-Yue ware and was also used at the Xicun kilns in Guangdong.

Shufu plates and bowls are always molded on the inside. Sometimes they are incised on the outside as well. Occasionally pouring vessels with flat, molded sides come on the market. Yuan Dehua pieces have stylized flowers, abstract floral shapes, fish shapes, and lotus leaves incised, carved, or molded on them (Plate 14).

In the Ming and Qing periods, when potters used it, the decoration consisted mostly of delicately incised flowers, fruits, or wave scrolls.

Except for the common incised circles at the top of some pieces and occasional vertical ribbing on the lower part of others, Sawankhalok white ware is generally plain. Vietnamese pieces are often plain also.

Spotted *qingbai*
double-gourd
pouring vessel

Dehua covered box with molded
decoration

BLUE-AND-WHITE WARE

History

Blue-and-white ceramics have blue or blackish-blue decoration on a white or off-white body. Recent archeological finds in China show that white stoneware with an underglaze blue decoration was made as early as the Tang dynasty, but it is very scarce and seems to have gone quickly out of production. It was only in the mid-fourteenth century, with the development of foreign trade, that the production of blue-and-white porcelain rose to commercial scale to meet the demand from the Middle East. Customers there wanted ceramics with motifs suited to their taste and, above all, in their favorite color.

The Persians had made use of cobalt blue to decorate ceramics but could not control the glazes and asked the

Blue-and-white plate with Islamic-style decoration. China. Ming dynasty. 30 cm across.

Chinese to do it for them. Even though the Chinese had known about cobalt blue for centuries, they had not made great use of it. For this new trade, they imported the pigment from the Middle East. Even they had trouble getting a clear color consistently. Many of their experiments were exported. Most experts consider that large-scale production of blue-and-white ware began in the second quarter of the fourteenth century.

Even when they had the color under better control, blue-and-white ware was made primarily for export. The Chinese may at first have considered it lavish and vulgar compared with the simplicity and sophistication of the monochrome wares of the Song period. When the imperial court began buying blue-and-white, however, even the domestic market was assured. Color gradually took pride of place over mass and shape. Celadon was then deposed as the export leader.

Jingdezhen, the main center for producing blue-and-white, became known internationally during the Ming and Qing periods. The new white porcelain body provided an ideal base for blue decoration. Some people think that blue-and-white export ware reached its artistic peak in the early fifteenth century. Actually, the technical peak was in the Qing period, but these ceramics lack the spontaneity of Ming blue-and-white ware. The operations were enormous. In the eighteenth century, there were reported to be more than a million people supporting 3,000 kilns.

Chinese blue-and-white styles have influenced ceramics internationally ever since. By the eighteenth century, much of China's output was destined for Europe, but it was also used all over Asia. The Willow Tree pattern was very popular everywhere. It is a nineteenth-century British transfer pattern—inspired by Chinese design—that was later taken up by the Chinese to meet the demand from Europe.

From the Ming period onward, blue-and-white ware has been used as everyday tableware in southeast Asia. The best known type is Shantou (Swatow), named after the port in southeast China from which the extensive products of that area were shipped (Plates 23a, 23b). Shantou ware was traded through the sixteenth and seventeenth centuries. It was made only in "export quality," a euphemism for "made in a hurry," and shipped to southeast Asia, India, the Middle East, and parts of Africa and Japan. It was collected rather than buried, coming, as it did, after the introduction of Islam and Christianity, which did not adopt the practice of grave furnishing. Another type, Canton ware (also known as Singapore, Hong Kong, Kitchen Ming, or Kitchen Qing ware) got its name because Canton (Guangzhou), Hong Kong, and Singapore were the chief ports through which this Ming tableware was shipped (Plates 22a, 22b). Canton ware is especially common in remote areas in the Philippines, where the Spanish could

Shantou (Swatow) plate with blue-and-white floral decoration. China. Ming dynasty. 31 cm across.

not enforce their edict against burying objects in graves. It is also plentiful in Thailand and Indonesia.

Another well-known style is called *Kraak* porcelain after the Portuguese word for the type of ship that often transported blue-and-white ware. The quality is too variable to generalize about these pieces. Only the style of decoration is consistent: the designs are placed in panels. Most *Kraak* ware went to Europe.

The Vietnamese also made beautiful blue-and-white ware, but they did not make as much as the Chinese, or for as long a time (Plate 20). They began production in the fourteenth century, the same time that production started in China. Over the next century or so they adopted Chinese designs, rendering them in a distinctive style. They entered the same markets, reaching the Philippines and Indonesia in the fifteenth century and fading from the scene several centuries later. The Japanese moved into the southeast Asian market in the eighteenth and nineteenth centuries.

Vietnamese blue-and-white covered box

Vietnamese bottle

Appearance

Shape

The Chinese tried to please their customers in the Middle East by imitating the shapes and motifs the latter knew from metal ware. They succeeded so well that urns, vases, and ewers formed in clay might be confused in shape with those made of brass. To the Middle East market also went enormous plates, for in those countries people ate together from one large, communal dish.

To southeast Asia the Chinese sent mass-produced blue-and-white plates and smaller dishes, covered boxes, bowls, jars with and without lids, jarlets, and pots. Water droppers and brush holders, accessories for the desks of Chinese scholars, were exported only if defective; they were for rituals and burials, not for calligraphy. Stem cups and small jars, often not too symmetrical, are common. Shantou ware was mostly plates (Plate 23), bowls, boxes, jars, and bottles. In Canton ware, plates and bowls are the most common.

The Vietnamese made an amazing range of shapes and styles—plates, saucers, vases, bowls, jarlets, large dishes, and covered boxes—which resemble underglaze black Sawankhalok pieces. Very few of the larger pieces for the Middle East market came to southeast Asia.

Body / Clay

In the Qing period the porcelain body became much whiter and thinner in weight than in the Yuan and Ming periods. One writer describes Ming blue-and-white porcelain as masculine and Qing blue-and-white as feminine. This refers to wares of the best quality; Shantou and Canton ware are both heavy, of coarse grey, buff, or white clay, and are often not symmetrical. The stoneware in Vietnamese pieces is grayish white, white, and buff (Plate 20).

Glaze

Qing glazes are usually thinner than Ming glazes. Seventeenth- and eighteenth-century dishes and plates sometimes had brown-glazed rims. Shantou ware has casually applied thick, milky glaze with some crackle.

Base / Footrim

The finish of many of the Ming pieces was short of perfection and they were often unnecessarily heavy. The feet were often poorly trimmed. Sometimes there was no footrim, especially in vases, and no glaze on the base. The famous hole-bottom style has no footrim. Rather, it has an indented base. In contrast, Qing-period pieces have glazed bases and are beautifully finished.

In Shantou ware, regardless of the quality, the footrims are thick and most of the bases are heavy. The bases feel gritty and sandy. They have picked up sand from the floor of the kiln during firing. Canton ware can be clearly identified by the same sandy base but also by a big unglazed ring on the inside. This clear ring prevented the pieces stacked one on top of another from fusing together during firing.

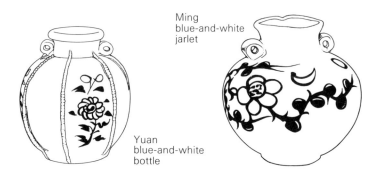

Ming blue-and-white jarlet

Yuan blue-and-white bottle

Vietnamese blue-and-white wares cannot be identified just by their feet: there are dozens of different shapes and styles. The surest sign of a Vietnamese piece, found on one third of the pieces produced as export ware, is the mysterious "chocolate bottom," an iron oxide wash on the base (Plate 19b). Some early pieces have five or six spur marks on the interior, or an unglazed center ring. Some bowls have a very high foot.

Decoration

Many early Chinese pieces catering to Islamic taste are almost entirely covered with decoration. The motifs are Chinese, but the density is definitely Islamic. Many later pieces, especially of Shantou ware, bear Arabic script, perhaps a quotation from the Koran. Dishes with nine squares containing script are common in Indonesia.

Decorations in this period include the old favorites: the lotus flower, the peony, and the chrysanthemum. Potters also liked flowers and plants, reeds, clouds, waves, and flaming pearls. Human figures appear, as well as pheasants and other birds, fish, and mythical creatures like flying horses or phoenixes. In the late Ming and early Qing porcelains, fanciful scenes came into fashion. Shading was used—dark blue for the outlines, and lighter shades inside. Jars usually had floral borders above and below the scenes.

Lotus-blossom motif

Dragons went on being used for centuries. Some people believe that dragons have five-clawed feet on imperial ware and fewer claws on less important pieces. The distinction should not be taken too seriously. Dragons with both three and five claws have been found on the same piece.

The early Ming blue-and-white pieces made for domestic and export use have an appealing spontaneity. The painting is free although, sometimes, it is coarse and imprecise (Plate 22). The cobalt blue coloring, which is often blackish or watery, appears to float under the glaze. Later painters carefully filled in an outlined pattern and the result is stiff and artificial. In the late sixteenth century, the quality of export ware deteriorated. The blue became blackish again later in the Ming period because potters did not take enough care.

In the early fifteenth century, reign marks appeared for the first time, but not on every piece. They are highly unreliable guides to the date of manufacture.

On the best pieces of Shantou ware, the painting is delicate and precise, though not stiff: on lesser pieces the painting is casual, loose, and watery (Plate 23). Most of the

Dragon on
blue-and-white jar

pieces are blue-and-white. Green, red, and other colors are sometimes added over the glaze or are used alone. (*See* the **Ware of Other Colors** section.) Shantou decoration is usually applied under the thick, off-white glaze, primarily on plates and bowls. The designs—animals, birds, sprays, little ships, and landscapes—often leave a good deal more white showing than the more heavily decorated ware of the Yuan and early Ming periods. The carp pattern began its rise to the popularity it still enjoys. A few plates have the split pagoda design in which the pagoda looks as though it has been cleaved vertically by the stroke of an axe.

On Canton ware, the painting is informal but attractive, with casually placed rectangular patterns stamped around the cavetto, freestyle trailing leaves, central floral medallions, and, on the outside, perhaps only a few lines.

Early in the Yuan and Ming periods, the white background had a bluish cast. This disappeared toward the end of the Ming period. In the Qing era, both the white and the blue became much clearer. The decoration became more precise and the finish cleaner (Plate 21). In the best Qing pieces the white is very white and the clear blue design ap-

Spray of trailing
morning glories

pears to float between the transparent surface glaze and the clay body.

Early Vietnamese blue-and-white ware had simple designs. A more elaborate painting style appears to have been introduced during the Ming invasion, 1406–27. Even so, the Vietnamese imposed their own style. Sharply defined, subtly shaded patterns usually fill more of the surface of the best quality pieces than one finds on good Chinese pieces. Covered jars have panels of floral decoration, surrounded by blocks of geometric patterns (Plate 20). On other shapes, Vietnamese artists drew fish, lotus blossoms, peonies, chrysanthemums, phoenixes, and dragons.

Vietnamese blue-and-white dish

WARE OF OTHER COLORS

Just when long exposure to ceramics begins to build confidence, suddenly pieces appear that do not fit any of the categories—a Ming covered box in green and yellow, for instance.

Though many potters experimented with color, it was mostly Chinese potters who produced the varied styles that do not fit into any of the larger categories or, later on, became categories themselves. Two of the most famous—and most valuable—are Jun ware and Guan ware.

Jun ware generally has a rich, glowing, powder blue glaze, sometimes with splashes or streaks of red or purple. The shapes of Jun ware are simple; the pieces are usually undecorated. It was made in the north of China from the Song possibly to the early Ming period and was not exported.

Guan ware, an imperial ware of the southern Song period, has several unusual qualities. What one notices first is the very heavy crackle; next, that the glaze is thicker than the body. As in Jun ware, the shapes are simple, but Guan colors are subtle blues, greens, or off-whites. True Guan

Guan jar with crackle

ware is hard to identify because potters copied its techniques in the Qing period. Unlike the original Guan ware, these later pieces were exported.

Monochrome Ware

The Chinese made pieces in copper red, blue, turquoise, and green. After flourishing in the early Ming period, monochrome copper red ware disappeared in the sixteenth century, only to reappear over a century later (Plate 24). Plain blue was rare in the fifteenth century but became more common in the sixteenth century. Turquoise became popular in the sixteenth century, as did copper green, imperial yellow, and purple: ox blood (*sang de boeuf*) came into use in the mid-seventeenth century. Sometimes the insides of these pieces have white glazing. By the seventeenth century, the pieces are flawlessly manufactured, but lack the freshness of earlier hand-crafting.

Wares in Red and Green and . . .

Some Chinese pieces have an underglaze copper red decoration. The patterns look much like those used in blue-and-white, but underglaze red pieces are rarer. Red was first used for decoration on *qingbai* ware. In the mid-fourteenth century, only a few pieces were made because copper red was even harder to control than cobalt blue. The red tended to melt into the overglaze or come out grey or brown. By the late fourteenth century, however, more red-and-white ware was being made than blue-and-white ware. Perhaps at that point cobalt blue was in short supply.

Philippine and Indonesian excavations have yielded very few pieces of fourteenth-century underglaze red ware. Just south of Manila, only one red decorated piece has been found for every thirty or forty blue-and-white pieces. In other locations, no red might be found at all. By the fifteenth century, the Chinese had mastered red underglazing, but in the sixteenth century copper red disappeared. It was replaced by a warm, overglaze orange-red made from iron. Copper red underglaze reappeared only late in the seventeenth century.

Most of the export wares are small and come from the Ming period. Yuan pieces are very rare. Ming pieces include small jarlets, rounded and square. Many were carelessly potted and finished. Early Qing pieces were done very well.

The small pieces are decorated with trailing red vines, scrolls, and floral sprays. Many pieces have beading as well. Larger pieces made use of baselines, a series of lines depicting the ground.

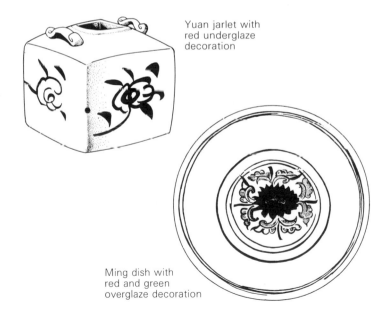

Yuan jarlet with red underglaze decoration

Ming dish with red and green overglaze decoration

Overglaze Decoration

It is likely that the Chinese invented enamel glazes. In the late fifteenth and early sixteenth centuries, coffee brown, red, blue, green, and yellow enamel decoration became common. Enamel yellow was sometime applied over the blue-and-white design. By the Qing period enamel glazing was well refined.

In the fifteenth and sixteenth centuries, the Vietnamese added red, green, and sometimes yellow painting to the traditional white ware with underglaze blue. They put the blue underneath and the other colors on top. The Chinese also made pieces in these styles: Shantou ware is an example. Pieces totally underglazed have survived better because any decoration over the glaze is likely to erode away during long burial. On many overglazed pieces that look bright now, the pattern has been retraced. On true heirloom pieces, of course, the pattern remains because it was never buried. Both types are found in southeast Asia.

During these centuries the decoration on porcelain became more brilliantly colored. By the early Qing dynasty, red, yellow, green, blue, and purple could be found all together on one piece. The blue gradually emerged from under the glaze to become over-the-glaze enamel. Many large jars with polychrome decoration are found in Indonesia.

During the Qing period, Chinese potters continued making blue-and-white ware and the other traditional styles for export. They also began making many new styles as a result of the expanding demand from Europe. Pieces known to have been made for a Western market are described as "Chinese export ware." The designs are either Chinese with some European influences or entirely European. The porcelain is often decorated with flowers, birds, or armorial designs. Many styles are called by French names—*famille* verte, jaune, rose, or *noire*. Some was sold, as well, in southeast Asia.

Two enamel wares, both densely decorated, were produced in China solely for specific markets in southeast Asia. Nonya ware was made for ceremonial use by Straits of Malacca Chinese families in the late nineteenth and early twentieth centuries. It has brightly colored, strong but orderly patterns. The colorful Bencharong enamel ware was made for the Thai market. Modern copies abound in Thailand.

EXPLORATIONS

WHERE TO LOOK

Major Asian Museums

China
National Palace Museum, Beijing
Shanghai Museum, Shanghai

Hong Kong
Fung Ping Shan Museum, University of Hong Kong
Hong Kong Museum of Art
Hong Kong Museum of History

Indonesia
Adam Malik Collection, Museum Keramik, Jakarta
Museum Pusat, Jakarta

Japan
Idemitsu Museum, Tokyo
Tokyo National Museum, Tokyo

Korea
Duksoo Palace Museum of Fine Arts, Seoul
National Museum of Korea, Seoul
Toksu Palace Museum, Seoul

Malaysia
Museum of the Arts of Asia, Kuala Lumpur
Museum Negara, Kuala Lumpur
University of Malaya Museum, Petaling Jaya

Myanmar (Burma)
National Museum of Art and Archaeology, Yangon
(Rangoon)

Philippines
National Museum of the Philippines: Manila; and the
Regional Museum, Butuan, Mindanao
Villa Escudero, San Pablo, Laguna

Singapore
National University
National Museum

Taiwan
National Palace Museum, Taipei

Thailand
Chiang Mai National Museum
Jim Thompson's Thai House, Bangkok
National Museum, Bangkok
Sukhotai Provincial Museum

Ceramic Displays Outside Asia

Australia
Art Gallery of South Australia, Adelaide
National Gallery of Victoria, Melbourne

Canada
Royal Ontario Museum, Toronto

Continental Europe
Benaki Museum, Athens, Greece
Musée Guimet, Paris, France
Museum für Östasiatische Kunst, Cologne, FRG
Museum of Decorative Art, Copenhagen, Denmark
Museum of Far Eastern Antiquities, Stockholm, Sweden
Princessehof Museum, Leeuwarden, the Netherlands

Great Britain
   Ashmolean Museum, Oxford
   Gulbenkian Museum of Oriental Art, Durham
   Percival David Foundation of Chinese Art, University of
      London
   Victoria and Albert Museum, London

Middle East
   Iran Bastan Museum, Teheran, Iran
   National Museum, Damascus, Syria
   Topkapi Saray, Istanbul, Turkey

United States
   The Asia Society, New York City
   Asian Art Museum, San Francisco
   Chicago Art Institute
   Cleveland Museum of Art
   Denver Art Museum
   Freer Gallery of Art, Smithsonian Institution,
      Washington
   Honolulu Academy of Arts
   Indianapolis Museum of Art
   Metropolitan Museum of Art, New York City
   Museum of Anthropology, University of Michigan, Ann
      Arbor
   Museum of Art, Columbus, Ohio
   Museum of Fine Arts, Boston
   Nelson-Atkins Museum of Art, Kansas City, Missouri
   Oriental Institute Museum, University of Chicago
   Philadelphia Art Museum
   Philbrook Art Center, Tulsa
   University of Indiana Art Museum, Bloomington

WHAT TO LOOK FOR

Getting Started

Go to as many antique and ceramics stores as possible. Handle the pieces, ask the dealers questions, get the feel. Keep going back. Keep looking and touching.

Haunt museums. Seek out public and private collections and arrange invitations to view them, preferably with a knowledgeable guide.

Find some pieces in a style you really like. Study them and study about them carefully. You cannot master the whole field.

The General Checkup

Look at ceramics in strong daylight. Carry a magnifying glass to examine every inch carefully.

To identify a piece, decide which major category it fits into—celadon, brown ware, etc. Then check the shape, potting, base/footrim, glaze, and decoration against the characteristics of that type. Pay most attention to the base and the footrim, which often give the best clues to the origin of a piece.

Body

Turn the piece slowly in your hand and revolve it on a table to see if it is crooked, sagging, or off-center. The best pieces stand symmetrically.

Look around the whole piece for variations in the thickness of the clay. Variations are most noticeable around the lip. The best pieces are of uniform thickness.

Consider the weight. If a piece is extraordinarily heavy for its size, it may be crudely made.

Be sure that the lid fits the base. Check that the glazes are similar. Rotate the piece carefully to ensure that any pattern matches on both sections. Covered boxes are often mismatched.

Glazes

Look for glazes that are smooth, that catch the light. Celadons especially should have a warm glow. Avoid dull glazes and glazes that have dull patches, blotches, or streaks that do not appear to be intentional or that look unattractive.

Feel the glaze. Some pieces are very dull, rough to the touch, have little pockmarks, or sound scratchy and catch if you rub them on your clothes. On these, the decoration may have faded or eroded away under chemical action while the piece was buried. It is often tempting to buy such pieces. Think twice. They don't give the lasting pleasure given by a piece in good condition.

Look for blemishes on the surface—bits of clay stuck to the body, little cuts in the clay, pockmarks in the glaze, hairline cracks, unglazed spots. These decrease the appeal and therefore the value of a piece.

Look for uniform color. That indicates correct firing.

Look for clear, precise painting. Runny or watery painting is usually less desirable.

Consider how much of the piece is glazed. The bigger the unglazed area, the more likely the piece was sloppily mass-produced.

Look at the clarity of the glaze. The clearer the glaze, the earlier the piece. Glazes on many export pieces became milky in the Ming period. There is an exception to this rule of thumb, however. If glazing is clear and painting is also very precise, the piece is likely late, probably made in the Qing period.

Repairs

Most well done repairs and enhancements of decoration are hard to detect.

Rub a coin around the rim of a plate or bowl to see if it has been repaired. If there is no ringing sound or if the pitch changes, then it is likely there has been some restoration.

Give the piece a flick of your finger. A ringing sound usually indicates that a piece is undamaged and of good quality.

Often a plate will have been broken in large pieces and reglued. Look for big repairs as well as small ones and small chips. Plates are often broken in big pieces—perhaps by accident, perhaps deliberately before burial in a grave—and some have been carefully reglued.

Decoration can be repainted. This is especially easy on earthenware pieces and pieces with overglaze decoration. Monochrome pieces, especially white ware, can have color added. More colors can be added to blue-and-white ware.

Be especially suspicious of the lips of jars. If they are too smooth or different in texture or color or sheen from the body, they have most likely been repaired.

Assume that any spout has been repaired or remade. If you can be persuaded that it is original, you may have a treasure.

Missing parts are sometimes replaced with plain clay, left unpainted. Many people consider this preferable to a disguised repair because it shows no attempt is being made to fool the buyer. There is a trend to leaving pieces unrepaired, to show that nothing is being hidden.

Fakes

No matter how cautious you are, the chances are good that at some time you will buy a fake. Fakers are getting smarter as prices for old ceramics increase, which means that fakes are very hard to detect. They will even break and repair a new piece, so that it appears to have been around a long time. Nowadays, even the experts are deceived.

Antique ceramic styles have long been reproduced in Taiwan, Hong Kong, Singapore, and Thailand, but not always to deceive; nevertheless, the products often appear on the market as antiques. These pieces are sold all over southeast Asia. In Jakarta antique stores, for instance, there are so many Sawankhalok covered boxes that it is hard to believe they are all genuine.

To say that a piece is a fake does not necessarily mean that it was newly made from scratch. Pieces can be rebuilt, redecorated, reglazed, and even refired. Kiln wasters and shards can be pieced together, the joints being carefully concealed. Be sceptical about Khmer pots: they may be made from the hoards of shards available. In such cases, the proportions may not be pleasing.

Good glazes, especially clear glazes, are very hard to fake.

Good buys

If you decide to become a collector, even in a small way, think about the shape your collection might take. Will it be all blue-and-white? Will it be one of each major style? Will it be just boxes?

Buy from an established dealer, unless you are very knowledgeable. If you become a good customer, you can likely make it a condition of the sale that you can exchange a piece if you start to have doubts about it or your taste changes.

Experts advise against buying an object that has been repaired. Ignore the experts and buy it anyway if you love it and the price is one you are willing to pay. The resale value may be low, but the pleasure of looking at a beautiful piece can be lifelong.

Take your time buying, especially with major pieces. Some people find it wise to take an expert friend along to give a second opinion. Many dealers are willing to leave a piece with a likely buyer for a day or two.

Don't pay too much attention to any sort of museum authentication sticker that clearly can be transferred from one piece to another. You can always ask a dealer for a certificate attesting to the authenticity of a piece you like. Or get in touch with a local museum yourself before paying for a piece.

There is no reason to believe that good pieces will be cheaper outside big cities. Sometimes country dealers take pieces on consignment from dealers in a city; they may even ask for more money than the city dealer's price. City dealers also consign inferior pieces—pots with mismatched lids, for instance—to country dealers, who then try to sell them to less knowledgeable customers.

Don't expect to find hidden treasures. Most dealers know precisely the value of what they have. Thus, bargains are rare. Competition for good pieces is heavy, and there are many wealthy buyers.

Don't hesitate to bargain: no dealer will reduce a price unless you ask. But shop around first to get a good idea of what you think a fair price might be. In other words, don't try to buy a vase for half of what you know to be a fair price; if you succeed, you will truly have gotten what you paid for.

Buy from established dealers with valid licenses, which assures (almost always) authenticity. Then any claims you may have later concerning the attribution of a piece may be dealt with officially.

WHAT TO READ

Many of these books can be found in the museums listed under **Where to Look** or in the collections of the Oriental Ceramic Societies and Muscum Volunteers groups in major Asian cities. Many of the more recent books are available in book stores.

Introductory

General

Brown, Roxanna M. *The Ceramics of South East Asia: Their Dating and Identification.* Kuala Lumpur: Oxford University Press, 1977. Excellent black-and-white photographs.

Encyclopedia Britannica. Excellent basic information.

Gorham, Hazel H. *Japanese and Oriental Ceramics.* Tokyo: Charles E. Tuttle Company, 1971. Reprint of a classic work, an invaluable guide.

Guy, John S. *Oriental Trade Ceramics in South-East Asia: Ninth to Sixteenth Centuries.* Singapore: Oxford University Press, 1986. Good general introduction. Catalogue for exhibit in Australia. Good pictures.

Rooney, Dawn F. *Folk Pottery in South-East Asia.* Singapore: Oxford University Press, 1987. One of the volumes in Oxford's excellent and low-priced "Images of Asia" series. Approach is different but worthwhile.

Southeast Asian Ceramic Society, Singapore. *Chinese Celadons and Other Related Wares in Southeast Asia.* Singapore: Arts Orientalis, 1979. Wonderful color pictures. Several chapters excellent.

China

Harrisson, Barbara. *Swatow in het Princessehof Leeuwarden*. Leeuwarden, the Netherlands: Gemeetelijk Museum Het Princessehof, 1979. The catalogue of possibly the largest collection in the world of Swatow ware.

Hayashiya, Seizo, and Gakuji Hasebe. *Chinese Ceramics*. Tokyo: Charles E. Tuttle Company, 1966. Now out-of-print classic that can be found in libraries. Good general introduction.

Medley, Margaret. *The Chinese Potter, A Practical History of Chinese Ceramics*. Ithaca: Cornell University Press, 1976. Advanced material, but written in a straightforward, readable fashion.

———. *Illustrated Catalogue of Celadon Wares*. London: Percival David Foundation of Chinese Art (University of London), 1977. Excellent introduction, good photos.

The Oriental Ceramic Society of Hong Kong. *Jingdezhen Wares: The Yuan Evolution*. Hong Kong: Fung Ping Shan Museum (University of Hong Kong), 1984. Beautiful pictures and interesting papers.

Southeast Asian Ceramic Society, West Malaysian Chapter. *Nonya Ware and Kitchen Ch'ing: Ceremonial and Domestic Pottery of the Nineteenth and Twentieth Centuries Commonly Found in Malaysia*. Kuala Lumpur: Oxford University Press, 1981.

Vainker S.J. *Chinese Pottery and Porcelain: From Prehistory to the Present*. London: The British Museum Press, 1991.

Valenstein, Suzanne G. *A Handbook of Chinese Ceramics*. New York: The Metropolitan Museum, 1975. Museum catalogue. Good general introduction and pictures.

Indonesia

Adhyatman, Sumaruh. *Antique Ceramics Found in Indonesia: Various Uses and Origins.* London: Hugh Moss (Publishing) Ltd., 1973. Excellent.

Japan

Moes, Robert. *The Brooklyn Museum Japanese Ceramics.* Brooklyn: The Brooklyn Museum, 1979. Catalogue.

Munsterberg, Hugo. *The Ceramic Art of Japan: A Handbook for Collectors.* Tokyo: Charles E. Tuttle Company, 1964. Over 250 excellent illustrations with informative text.

Reichel, Friedrich. *Early Japanese Porcelain in the Dresden Collection.* London: Orbis Publishing, 1982. Excellent overview and detail from the late sixteenth century on.

Till, Barry and Paula Swart. *The Flowering of Japanese Ceramic Art: Late Sixteenth Century to the Present.* Victoria, BC: Art Gallery of Greater Victoria, 1983. Catalogue. Concise, simple introduction.

Kampuchea (see *Thailand*)

Korea

Akaboshi, Goro, and Heiichiro Nakamaru. *Five Centuries of Korean Ceramics: Pottery and Porcelain of the Yi Dynasty.* New York, Tokyo, and Kyoto: Weatherhill/ Tankosha, 1955.

Myanmar (Burma) (see *Thailand*)

Philippines

Locsin, Leandro, and Cecilia Locsin. *Oriental Ceramics*

Discovered in the Philippines. Tokyo: Charles E. Tuttle Company, 1967. The first book on the subject. An out-of-print collector's item. The many pictures are helpful. Some information out of date, but essential background reading.

Oriental Ceramics Society of the Philippines. *Guangdong Ceramics from Butuan and other Philippine Sites.* Manila: Oriental Ceramics Society of the Philippines/Oxford University Press, 1989.

Peralta, Jesus T. *Kayamanan: Pottery and Ceramics from the Arturo de Santos Collection.* Manila: Central Bank of the Philippines, 1982. The Kayamanan series is excellent. This one displays well what has been found in the Philippines.

Thailand

Shaw, J.C. *Introducing Thai Ceramics, also Burmese and Khmer.* Chiang Mai: Craftsman Press, 1987. Useful, clearly presented information.

Stratton, Carol, and Miriam McNair Scott. *The Art of Sukhotai, Thailand's Golden Age.* Kuala Lumpur: Oxford University Press, 1981. One chapter of this survey is on ceramics. Attractive presentation.

Vietnam

Young, Carol M., Marie-France Dupoizat, and Elizabeth W. Lane. *Vietnamese Ceramics, with an Illustrated Catalogue of the Exhibition Organized by the Southeast Asian Ceramic Society at the National Museum, Singapore in June 1982.* Singapore: Southeast Asian Ceramic Society/Oxford University Press, 1982.

Advanced

Garner, Sir Harry. *Oriental Blue and White*. London: Faber and Faber, 1970.

Gray, Basil. *Sung Porcelain and Stoneware*. London: Faber and Faber, 1984.

Hobson, R.L. *The Wares of the Ming Dynasty*. Tokyo: Charles E. Tuttle Company, 1962. Reprint of one of the primary sources of information on Ming ware.

Li Zhiyan and Cheng Wen. *Chinese Pottery and Porcelain*. Beijing: Foreign Languages Press, 1984.

Medley, Margaret. *A Handbook of Chinese Art for Collectors and Students*. London: Bell and Hyman, 1977.

The National Museum, Singapore. Kendis: A Guide to the Collections in the National Museum, Singapore. Singapore: National Museum, 1984.

Spinks, Charles Nelson. *The Ceramic Wares of Thailand*. Bangkok: Siam Society, 1965 (revised 1978). One of the great experts. Detailed and authoritative in most areas. Out of date in places.

Treager, Mary. *Song Ceramics*. New York: Rizzoli International Publications, Inc., 1982. Very detailed.

Willetts, William. *Ceramic Art of Southeast Asia*. Singapore: The Southeast Asian Ceramics Society, 1971. Catalogue. Text detailed. Black-and-white pictures with useful descriptions.

Yeo, S.T., and Jean Martin. *Chinese Blue and White Ceramics*. Singapore: Arts Orientalis, 1978. Catalogue of exhibition by the Southeast Asian Ceramics Society and the National Museum of Singapore, 1978. Text detailed. Hundreds of beautiful pictures.

Elizabeth Wilson is a writer who lived in the Philippines for three years. She has been looking at Oriental ceramics all her life. Toronto, Canada, where she lives, has one of the best collections of Chinese antiquities outside China. She has taken pottery courses in Toronto and Oakland, California. During work and travel in Southeast Asia, she studied Oriental ceramics in China, Indonesia, and Thailand.

Her book, *A Pocket Guide to Oriental Ceramics in the Philippines* was published by Bookmark, Manila in 1988.